C000084542

Multisourcing Integration
Complete Self-Assessment Guide

The guidance in this Self-Assessment is based on Multisourcing Integration best practices and standards in business process architecture, design and quality management. The guidance is also based on the professional judgment of the individual collaborators listed in the Acknowledgments.

Notice of rights

Trademarks

Table of Contents

About The Art of Service

The Art of Service, Business Process Architects since 2000, is dedicated to helping stakeholders achieve excellence.

Defining, designing, creating, and implementing a process to solve a stakeholders challenge or meet an objective is the most valuable role… In EVERY group, company, organization and department.

Unless you're talking a one-time, single-use project, there should be a process. Whether that process is managed and implemented by humans, AI, or a combination of the two, it needs to be designed by someone with a complex enough perspective to ask the right questions.

Someone capable of asking the right questions and step back and say, 'What are we really trying to accomplish here? And is there a different way to look at it?'

With The Art of Service's Standard Requirements Self-Assessments, we empower people who can do just that — whether their title is marketer, entrepreneur, manager, salesperson, consultant, Business Process Manager, executive assistant, IT Manager, CIO etc... —they are the people who rule the future. They are people who watch the process as it happens, and ask the right questions to make the process work better.

Contact us when you need any support with this Self-Assessment and any help with templates, blue-prints and examples of standard documents you might need:

http://theartofservice.com
service@theartofservice.com

Acknowledgments

This checklist was developed under the auspices of The Art of Service, chaired by Gerardus Blokdyk.

Representatives from several client companies participated in the preparation of this Self-Assessment.

In addition, we are thankful for the design and printing services provided.

Included Resources - how to access

Included with your purchase of the book is the Multisourcing Integration Self-Assessment Spreadsheet Dashboard which contains all questions and Self-Assessment areas and auto-generates insights, graphs, and project RACI planning - all with examples to get you started right away.

How? Simply send an email to
access@theartofservice.com
with this books' title in the subject to get the Multisourcing Integration Self Assessment Tool right away.

You will receive the following contents with New and Updated specific criteria:

• The latest quick edition of the book in PDF

• The latest complete edition of the book in PDF, which criteria correspond to the criteria in...

• The Self-Assessment Excel Dashboard, and...

• Example pre-filled Self-Assessment Excel Dashboard to get familiar with results generation

• In-depth specific Checklists covering the topic

• Project management checklists and templates to assist with implementation

INCLUDES LIFETIME SELF ASSESSMENT UPDATES

Every self assessment comes with Lifetime Updates and Lifetime Free Updated Books. Lifetime Updates is an industry-first feature which allows you to receive verified self assessment updates, ensuring you always have the most accurate information at your fingertips.

Get it now- you will be glad you did - do it now, before you forget.

Send an email to **access@theartofservice.com** with this books' title in the subject to get the Multisourcing Integration Self Assessment Tool right away.

Your feedback is invaluable to us

If you recently bought this book, we would love to hear from you! You can do this by writing a review on amazon (or the online store where you purchased this book) about your last purchase! As part of our continual service improvement process, we love to hear real client experiences and feedback.

How does it work?
To post a review on Amazon, just log in to your account and click on the Create Your Own Review button (under Customer Reviews) of the relevant product page. You can find examples of product reviews in Amazon. If you purchased from another online store, simply follow their procedures.

What happens when I submit my review?
Once you have submitted your review, send us an email at review@theartofservice.com with the link to your review so we can properly thank you for your feedback.

Purpose of this Self-Assessment

This Self-Assessment has been developed to improve understanding of the requirements and elements of Multisourcing Integration, based on best practices and standards in business process architecture, design and quality management.

It is designed to allow for a rapid Self-Assessment to determine how closely existing management practices and procedures correspond to the elements of the Self-Assessment.

The criteria of requirements and elements of Multisourcing Integration have been rephrased in the format of a Self-Assessment questionnaire, with a seven-criterion scoring system, as explained in this document.

In this format, even with limited background knowledge of

Multisourcing Integration, a manager can quickly review existing operations to determine how they measure up to the standards. This in turn can serve as the starting point of a 'gap analysis' to identify management tools or system elements that might usefully be implemented in the organization to help improve overall performance.

How to use the Self-Assessment

On the following pages are a series of questions to identify to what extent your Multisourcing Integration initiative is complete in comparison to the requirements set in standards.

To facilitate answering the questions, there is a space in front of each question to enter a score on a scale of '1' to '5'.

1 Strongly Disagree

2 Disagree

3 Neutral

4 Agree

5 Strongly Agree

Read the question and rate it with the following in front of mind:

'In my belief,
the answer to this question is clearly defined'.

There are two ways in which you can choose to interpret this statement;
1. how aware are you that the answer to the question is clearly defined
2. for more in-depth analysis you can choose to gather

evidence and confirm the answer to the question. This obviously will take more time, most Self-Assessment users opt for the first way to interpret the question and dig deeper later on based on the outcome of the overall Self-Assessment.

A score of '1' would mean that the answer is not clear at all, where a '5' would mean the answer is crystal clear and defined. Leave emtpy when the question is not applicable or you don't want to answer it, you can skip it without affecting your score. Write your score in the space provided.

After you have responded to all the appropriate statements in each section, compute your average score for that section, using the formula provided, and round to the nearest tenth. Then transfer to the corresponding spoke in the Multisourcing Integration Scorecard on the second next page of the Self-Assessment.

Your completed Multisourcing Integration Scorecard will give you a clear presentation of which Multisourcing Integration areas need attention.

Multisourcing Integration Scorecard Example

Example of how the finalized Scorecard can look like:

Multisourcing Integration Scorecard

Your Scores:

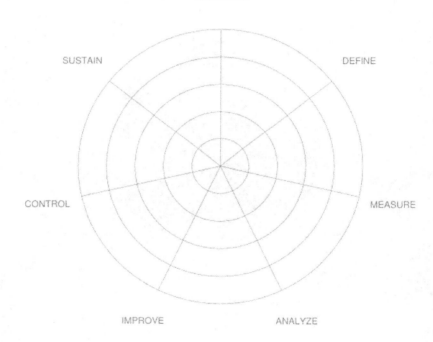

BEGINNING OF THE SELF-ASSESSMENT:

CRITERION #1: RECOGNIZE

INTENT: Be aware of the need for change. Recognize that there is an unfavorable variation, problem or symptom.

In my belief, the answer to this question is clearly defined:

5 Strongly Agree

4 Agree

3 Neutral

2 Disagree

1 Strongly Disagree

1. Are employees recognized or rewarded for performance that demonstrates the highest levels of integrity?
<--- Score

2. Are you dealing with any of the same issues today as yesterday? What can you do about this?
<--- Score

3. Who needs to know about multisourcing integration?

<--- Score

4. Are there recognized multisourcing integration problems?

<--- Score

5. What are the clients issues and concerns?

<--- Score

6. What is the problem or issue?

<--- Score

7. For your multisourcing integration project, identify and describe the business environment, is there more than one layer to the business environment?

<--- Score

8. As a sponsor, customer or management, how important is it to meet goals, objectives?

<--- Score

9. Who needs what information?

<--- Score

10. How are training requirements identified?

<--- Score

11. What are the timeframes required to resolve each of the issues/problems?

<--- Score

12. What needs to stay?

<--- Score

13. What multisourcing integration events should you attend?
<--- Score

14. Think about the people you identified for your multisourcing integration project and the project responsibilities you would assign to them, what kind of training do you think they would need to perform these responsibilities effectively?
<--- Score

15. What situation(s) led to this multisourcing integration Self Assessment?
<--- Score

16. What is the extent or complexity of the multisourcing integration problem?
<--- Score

17. How are the multisourcing integration's objectives aligned to the group's overall stakeholder strategy?
<--- Score

18. What resources or support might you need?
<--- Score

19. Consider your own multisourcing integration project, what types of organizational problems do you think might be causing or affecting your problem, based on the work done so far?
<--- Score

20. What do you need to start doing?
<--- Score

21. Do you recognize multisourcing integration

achievements?
<--- Score

22. Are there any revenue recognition issues?
<--- Score

23. What is the recognized need?
<--- Score

24. What creative shifts do you need to take?
<--- Score

25. Will it solve real problems?
<--- Score

26. What extra resources will you need?
<--- Score

27. What is the smallest subset of the problem you
can usefully solve?
<--- Score

28. What multisourcing integration coordination do
you need?
<--- Score

29. Do you have/need 24-hour access to key
personnel?
<--- Score

**30. What are the minority interests and what
amount of minority interests can be recognized?**
<--- Score

31. How do you recognize an objection?
<--- Score

32. Do you need to avoid or amend any multisourcing integration activities?
<--- Score

33. To what extent would your organization benefit from being recognized as a award recipient?
<--- Score

34. Are there any specific expectations or concerns about the multisourcing integration team, multisourcing integration itself?
<--- Score

35. Are problem definition and motivation clearly presented?
<--- Score

36. How does it fit into your organizational needs and tasks?
<--- Score

37. To what extent does each concerned units management team recognize multisourcing integration as an effective investment?
<--- Score

38. What does multisourcing integration success mean to the stakeholders?
<--- Score

39. Does the problem have ethical dimensions?
<--- Score

40. How many trainings, in total, are needed?
<--- Score

41. Who should resolve the multisourcing integration issues?
<--- Score

42. Are there regulatory / compliance issues?
<--- Score

43. How are you going to measure success?
<--- Score

44. What prevents you from making the changes you know will make you a more effective multisourcing integration leader?
<--- Score

45. Are your goals realistic? Do you need to redefine your problem? Perhaps the problem has changed or maybe you have reached your goal and need to set a new one?
<--- Score

46. When a multisourcing integration manager recognizes a problem, what options are available?
<--- Score

47. What do employees need in the short term?
<--- Score

48. Would you recognize a threat from the inside?
<--- Score

49. Where do you need to exercise leadership?
<--- Score

50. Is it needed?

<--- Score

51. Where is training needed?
<--- Score

52. Did you miss any major multisourcing integration issues?
<--- Score

53. What are the expected benefits of multisourcing integration to the stakeholder?
<--- Score

54. What activities does the governance board need to consider?
<--- Score

55. How can auditing be a preventative security measure?
<--- Score

56. What multisourcing integration capabilities do you need?
<--- Score

57. How do you take a forward-looking perspective in identifying multisourcing integration research related to market response and models?
<--- Score

58. Is the need for organizational change recognized?
<--- Score

59. Looking at each person individually – does every one have the qualities which are needed to work in

this group?
<--- Score

60. What vendors make products that address the multisourcing integration needs?
<--- Score

61. What are the multisourcing integration resources needed?
<--- Score

62. What would happen if multisourcing integration weren't done?
<--- Score

63. How do you identify the kinds of information that you will need?
<--- Score

64. What is the problem and/or vulnerability?
<--- Score

65. What should be considered when identifying available resources, constraints, and deadlines?
<--- Score

66. Does your organization need more multisourcing integration education?
<--- Score

67. Which needs are not included or involved?
<--- Score

68. Who else hopes to benefit from it?
<--- Score

69. What needs to be done?
<--- Score

70. What multisourcing integration problem should be solved?
<--- Score

71. What information do users need?
<--- Score

72. What are the stakeholder objectives to be achieved with multisourcing integration?
<--- Score

73. Are losses recognized in a timely manner?
<--- Score

74. Can management personnel recognize the monetary benefit of multisourcing integration?
<--- Score

75. How do you recognize an multisourcing integration objection?
<--- Score

76. What problems are you facing and how do you consider multisourcing integration will circumvent those obstacles?
<--- Score

77. What tools and technologies are needed for a custom multisourcing integration project?
<--- Score

78. How do you assess your multisourcing integration workforce capability and capacity

needs, including skills, competencies, and staffing levels?
<--- Score

79. What else needs to be measured?
<--- Score

80. What training and capacity building actions are needed to implement proposed reforms?
<--- Score

81. Who are your key stakeholders who need to sign off?
<--- Score

82. Who defines the rules in relation to any given issue?
<--- Score

83. What are your needs in relation to multisourcing integration skills, labor, equipment, and markets?
<--- Score

84. Is it clear when you think of the day ahead of you what activities and tasks you need to complete?
<--- Score

85. How do you identify subcontractor relationships?
<--- Score

86. Why is this needed?
<--- Score

87. Will new equipment/products be required to facilitate multisourcing integration delivery, for

example is new software needed?
<--- Score

88. Which information does the multisourcing integration business case need to include?
<--- Score

89. Who needs to know?
<--- Score

90. How much are sponsors, customers, partners, stakeholders involved in multisourcing integration? In other words, what are the risks, if multisourcing integration does not deliver successfully?
<--- Score

91. What is the multisourcing integration problem definition? What do you need to resolve?
<--- Score

92. Who needs budgets?
<--- Score

93. Are controls defined to recognize and contain problems?
<--- Score

94. Do you need different information or graphics?
<--- Score

95. Do you know what you need to know about multisourcing integration?
<--- Score

96. Are employees recognized for desired behaviors?
<--- Score

97. Is the quality assurance team identified?
<--- Score

98. Have you identified your multisourcing integration key performance indicators?
<--- Score

Add up total points for this section:
_ _ _ _ _ = Total points for this section

Divided by: _ _ _ _ _ _ (number of statements answered) = _ _ _ _ _ _
Average score for this section

Transfer your score to the multisourcing integration Index at the beginning of the Self-Assessment.

CRITERION #2: DEFINE:

INTENT: Formulate the stakeholder problem. Define the problem, needs and objectives.

In my belief, the answer to this question is clearly defined:

5 Strongly Agree

4 Agree

3 Neutral

2 Disagree

1 Strongly Disagree

1. Have all of the relationships been defined properly?
<--- Score

2. In what way can you redefine the criteria of choice clients have in your category in your favor?
<--- Score

3. Is there a completed, verified, and validated high-level 'as is' (not 'should be' or 'could be') stakeholder

process map?

<--- Score

4. Has the direction changed at all during the course of multisourcing integration? If so, when did it change and why?

<--- Score

5. How do you gather requirements?

<--- Score

6. How would you define the culture at your organization, how susceptible is it to multisourcing integration changes?

<--- Score

7. What system do you use for gathering multisourcing integration information?

<--- Score

8. What is the definition of success?

<--- Score

9. Do you have organizational privacy requirements?

<--- Score

10. Are accountability and ownership for multisourcing integration clearly defined?

<--- Score

11. Will team members perform multisourcing integration work when assigned and in a timely fashion?

<--- Score

12. Are resources adequate for the scope?

<--- Score

13. Is it clearly defined in and to your organization what you do?
<--- Score

14. What are the multisourcing integration tasks and definitions?
<--- Score

15. How do you keep key subject matter experts in the loop?
<--- Score

16. What is a worst-case scenario for losses?
<--- Score

17. What multisourcing integration requirements should be gathered?
<--- Score

18. Have all basic functions of multisourcing integration been defined?
<--- Score

19. Has a multisourcing integration requirement not been met?
<--- Score

20. How will variation in the actual durations of each activity be dealt with to ensure that the expected multisourcing integration results are met?
<--- Score

21. What gets examined?
<--- Score

22. What knowledge or experience is required?
<--- Score

23. What scope do you want your strategy to cover?
<--- Score

24. Are the multisourcing integration requirements testable?
<--- Score

25. Will a multisourcing integration production readiness review be required?
<--- Score

26. Has/have the customer(s) been identified?
<--- Score

27. Where can you gather more information?
<--- Score

28. Are customer(s) identified and segmented according to their different needs and requirements?
<--- Score

29. Do you all define multisourcing integration in the same way?
<--- Score

30. Has anyone else (internal or external to the group) attempted to solve this problem or a similar one before? If so, what knowledge can be leveraged from these previous efforts?
<--- Score

31. If substitutes have been appointed, have they been briefed on the multisourcing integration goals and received regular communications as to the progress to date?
<--- Score

32. What is the scope of the multisourcing integration effort?
<--- Score

33. How often are the team meetings?
<--- Score

34. How will the multisourcing integration team and the group measure complete success of multisourcing integration?
<--- Score

35. Who approved the multisourcing integration scope?
<--- Score

36. Are audit criteria, scope, frequency and methods defined?
<--- Score

37. What would be the goal or target for a multisourcing integration's improvement team?
<--- Score

38. What specifically is the problem? Where does it occur? When does it occur? What is its extent?
<--- Score

39. The political context: who holds power?
<--- Score

40. Has a team charter been developed and communicated?
<--- Score

41. Do you have a multisourcing integration success story or case study ready to tell and share?
<--- Score

42. Is the multisourcing integration scope manageable?
<--- Score

43. How have you defined all multisourcing integration requirements first?
<--- Score

44. Who defines (or who defined) the rules and roles?
<--- Score

45. How do you gather multisourcing integration requirements?
<--- Score

46. What information do you gather?
<--- Score

47. How do you build the right business case?
<--- Score

48. What is the worst case scenario?
<--- Score

49. What was the context?
<--- Score

50. Is there a multisourcing integration management charter, including stakeholder case, problem and goal statements, scope, milestones, roles and responsibilities, communication plan?
<--- Score

51. What customer feedback methods were used to solicit their input?
<--- Score

52. Does the scope remain the same?
<--- Score

53. Is there a critical path to deliver multisourcing integration results?
<--- Score

54. Is there a clear multisourcing integration case definition?
<--- Score

55. What key stakeholder process output measure(s) does multisourcing integration leverage and how?
<--- Score

56. What are the multisourcing integration use cases?
<--- Score

57. Is the team equipped with available and reliable resources?
<--- Score

58. Is there a completed SIPOC representation, describing the Suppliers, Inputs, Process, Outputs, and Customers?

<--- Score

59. How would you define multisourcing integration leadership?
<--- Score

60. Will team members regularly document their multisourcing integration work?
<--- Score

61. When is/was the multisourcing integration start date?
<--- Score

62. Do the problem and goal statements meet the SMART criteria (specific, measurable, attainable, relevant, and time-bound)?
<--- Score

63. What is out of scope?
<--- Score

64. Is multisourcing integration linked to key stakeholder goals and objectives?
<--- Score

65. Has everyone on the team, including the team leaders, been properly trained?
<--- Score

66. What are the dynamics of the communication plan?
<--- Score

67. What are the tasks and definitions?
<--- Score

68. How do you manage changes in multisourcing integration requirements?
<--- Score

69. What baselines are required to be defined and managed?
<--- Score

70. Are all requirements met?
<--- Score

71. Are approval levels defined for contracts and supplements to contracts?
<--- Score

72. Scope of sensitive information?
<--- Score

73. What are the record-keeping requirements of multisourcing integration activities?
<--- Score

74. Who is gathering multisourcing integration information?
<--- Score

75. What defines best in class?
<--- Score

76. How do you manage scope?
<--- Score

77. What happens if multisourcing integration's scope changes?
<--- Score

78. Is there any additional multisourcing integration definition of success?
<--- Score

79. What scope to assess?
<--- Score

80. What are the compelling stakeholder reasons for embarking on multisourcing integration?
<--- Score

81. Are different versions of process maps needed to account for the different types of inputs?
<--- Score

82. What are the boundaries of the scope? What is in bounds and what is not? What is the start point? What is the stop point?
<--- Score

83. Are task requirements clearly defined?
<--- Score

84. How can the value of multisourcing integration be defined?
<--- Score

85. How do you gather the stories?
<--- Score

86. Are there different segments of customers?
<--- Score

87. How does the multisourcing integration manager ensure against scope creep?

<--- Score

88. Is the improvement team aware of the different versions of a process: what they think it is vs. what it actually is vs. what it should be vs. what it could be?
<--- Score

89. What are the Roles and Responsibilities for each team member and its leadership? Where is this documented?
<--- Score

90. Has a project plan, Gantt chart, or similar been developed/completed?
<--- Score

91. What critical content must be communicated – who, what, when, where, and how?
<--- Score

92. Are required metrics defined, what are they?
<--- Score

93. What is the scope?
<--- Score

94. What are the requirements for audit information?
<--- Score

95. What are the rough order estimates on cost savings/opportunities that multisourcing integration brings?
<--- Score

96. How are consistent multisourcing integration definitions important?

<--- Score

97. Has your scope been defined?
<--- Score

98. What is in scope?
<--- Score

99. Are roles and responsibilities formally defined?
<--- Score

100. How do you hand over multisourcing integration context?
<--- Score

101. Has a high-level 'as is' process map been completed, verified and validated?
<--- Score

102. What sources do you use to gather information for a multisourcing integration study?
<--- Score

103. What intelligence can you gather?
<--- Score

104. What sort of initial information to gather?
<--- Score

105. What is the definition of multisourcing integration excellence?
<--- Score

106. Is the current 'as is' process being followed? If not, what are the discrepancies?
<--- Score

107. How did the multisourcing integration manager receive input to the development of a multisourcing integration improvement plan and the estimated completion dates/times of each activity?
<--- Score

108. When is the estimated completion date?
<--- Score

109. Is the team adequately staffed with the desired cross-functionality? If not, what additional resources are available to the team?
<--- Score

110. When are meeting minutes sent out? Who is on the distribution list?
<--- Score

111. What is out-of-scope initially?
<--- Score

112. Who are the multisourcing integration improvement team members, including Management Leads and Coaches?
<--- Score

113. Why are you doing multisourcing integration and what is the scope?
<--- Score

114. What multisourcing integration services do you require?
<--- Score

115. Is the scope of multisourcing integration

defined?
<--- Score

116. Are improvement team members fully trained on multisourcing integration?
<--- Score

117. Is multisourcing integration currently on schedule according to the plan?
<--- Score

118. What is the scope of the multisourcing integration work?
<--- Score

119. Is data collected and displayed to better understand customer(s) critical needs and requirements.
<--- Score

120. Is full participation by members in regularly held team meetings guaranteed?
<--- Score

121. What is the scope of multisourcing integration?
<--- Score

122. What constraints exist that might impact the team?
<--- Score

123. Are there any constraints known that bear on the ability to perform multisourcing integration work? How is the team addressing them?
<--- Score

124. Is scope creep really all bad news?
<--- Score

125. Is there regularly 100% attendance at the team meetings? If not, have appointed substitutes attended to preserve cross-functionality and full representation?
<--- Score

126. How do you think the partners involved in multisourcing integration would have defined success?
<--- Score

127. Has the multisourcing integration work been fairly and/or equitably divided and delegated among team members who are qualified and capable to perform the work? Has everyone contributed?
<--- Score

128. Is multisourcing integration required?
<--- Score

129. How is the team tracking and documenting its work?
<--- Score

130. What are the core elements of the multisourcing integration business case?
<--- Score

131. Have the customer needs been translated into specific, measurable requirements? How?
<--- Score

132. Has the improvement team collected the 'voice

of the customer' (obtained feedback – qualitative and quantitative)?
<--- Score

133. What is in the scope and what is not in scope?
<--- Score

134. How was the 'as is' process map developed, reviewed, verified and validated?
<--- Score

135. How do you catch multisourcing integration definition inconsistencies?
<--- Score

136. Is special multisourcing integration user knowledge required?
<--- Score

137. Does the team have regular meetings?
<--- Score

138. Are the multisourcing integration requirements complete?
<--- Score

139. What is the context?
<--- Score

140. What are (control) requirements for multisourcing integration Information?
<--- Score

Add up total points for this section:
_ _ _ _ _ = Total points for this section

Divided by: _____ (number of
statements answered) = _____
Average score for this section

Transfer your score to the multisourcing
integration Index at the beginning of
the Self-Assessment.

CRITERION #3: MEASURE:

INTENT: Gather the correct data. Measure the current performance and evolution of the situation.

In my belief, the answer to this question is clearly defined:

5 Strongly Agree

4 Agree

3 Neutral

2 Disagree

1 Strongly Disagree

1. How will costs be allocated?
<--- Score

2. What relevant entities could be measured?
<--- Score

3. How can you reduce costs?
<--- Score

4. Have design-to-cost goals been established?
<--- Score

5. How do you verify the multisourcing integration requirements quality?
<--- Score

6. What are the strategic priorities for this year?
<--- Score

7. How do you verify your resources?
<--- Score

8. Do you have any cost multisourcing integration limitation requirements?
<--- Score

9. What is your multisourcing integration quality cost segregation study?
<--- Score

10. What is an unallowable cost?
<--- Score

11. How are measurements made?
<--- Score

12. Are indirect costs charged to the multisourcing integration program?
<--- Score

13. Do you have a flow diagram of what happens?
<--- Score

14. Are multisourcing integration vulnerabilities categorized and prioritized?

<--- Score

15. What do you measure and why?
<--- Score

16. Who pays the cost?
<--- Score

17. The approach of traditional multisourcing integration works for detail complexity but is focused on a systematic approach rather than an understanding of the nature of systems themselves, what approach will permit your organization to deal with the kind of unpredictable emergent behaviors that dynamic complexity can introduce?
<--- Score

18. Are the units of measure consistent?
<--- Score

19. How do you measure efficient delivery of multisourcing integration services?
<--- Score

20. How do you measure variability?
<--- Score

21. What is your decision requirements diagram?
<--- Score

22. How sensitive must the multisourcing integration strategy be to cost?
<--- Score

23. How can you reduce the costs of obtaining inputs?

<--- Score

24. Do you effectively measure and reward individual and team performance?
<--- Score

25. What causes extra work or rework?
<--- Score

26. What happens if cost savings do not materialize?
<--- Score

27. Does the multisourcing integration task fit the client's priorities?
<--- Score

28. Have you included everything in your multisourcing integration cost models?
<--- Score

29. Who should receive measurement reports?
<--- Score

30. How will your organization measure success?
<--- Score

31. How can you manage cost down?
<--- Score

32. What would be a real cause for concern?
<--- Score

33. What methods are feasible and acceptable to estimate the impact of reforms?
<--- Score

34. What potential environmental factors impact the multisourcing integration effort?
<--- Score

35. What is the total fixed cost?
<--- Score

36. What does your operating model cost?
<--- Score

37. What causes investor action?
<--- Score

38. What does verifying compliance entail?
<--- Score

39. What evidence is there and what is measured?
<--- Score

40. Who is involved in verifying compliance?
<--- Score

41. How are you verifying it?
<--- Score

42. Where is the cost?
<--- Score

43. What can be used to verify compliance?
<--- Score

44. How will measures be used to manage and adapt?
<--- Score

45. What causes innovation to fail or succeed in your organization?

<--- Score

46. How are costs allocated?
<--- Score

47. What are the uncertainties surrounding estimates of impact?
<--- Score

48. How can you measure multisourcing integration in a systematic way?
<--- Score

49. Is the solution cost-effective?
<--- Score

50. What are the multisourcing integration investment costs?
<--- Score

51. How is the value delivered by multisourcing integration being measured?
<--- Score

52. What tests verify requirements?
<--- Score

53. Where is it measured?
<--- Score

54. How long to keep data and how to manage retention costs?
<--- Score

55. Why do you expend time and effort to implement measurement, for whom?

<--- Score

56. Does a multisourcing integration quantification method exist?
<--- Score

57. What are the costs?
<--- Score

58. Was a business case (cost/benefit) developed?
<--- Score

59. Are supply costs steady or fluctuating?
<--- Score

60. At what cost?
<--- Score

61. Does management have the right priorities among projects?
<--- Score

62. Are missed multisourcing integration opportunities costing your organization money?
<--- Score

63. How do you control the overall costs of your work processes?
<--- Score

64. Are there measurements based on task performance?
<--- Score

65. What are the costs of reform?
<--- Score

66. How do you verify and develop ideas and innovations?

<--- Score

67. Are the multisourcing integration benefits worth its costs?

<--- Score

68. What are you verifying?

<--- Score

69. What are the multisourcing integration key cost drivers?

<--- Score

70. Are you taking your company in the direction of better and revenue or cheaper and cost?

<--- Score

71. How do you quantify and qualify impacts?

<--- Score

72. Are actual costs in line with budgeted costs?

<--- Score

73. Do you aggressively reward and promote the people who have the biggest impact on creating excellent multisourcing integration services/ products?

<--- Score

74. Are there competing multisourcing integration priorities?

<--- Score

75. How much does it cost?
<--- Score

76. How will success or failure be measured?
<--- Score

77. What are the costs of delaying multisourcing integration action?
<--- Score

78. What does losing customers cost your organization?
<--- Score

79. What are the types and number of measures to use?
<--- Score

80. Do you verify that corrective actions were taken?
<--- Score

81. Has a cost center been established?
<--- Score

82. What could cause delays in the schedule?
<--- Score

83. What are allowable costs?
<--- Score

84. What is the total cost related to deploying multisourcing integration, including any consulting or professional services?
<--- Score

85. What are hidden multisourcing integration quality

costs?

<--- Score

86. How will effects be measured?

<--- Score

87. Did you tackle the cause or the symptom?

<--- Score

88. Have you made assumptions about the shape of the future, particularly its impact on your customers and competitors?

<--- Score

89. Why do the measurements/indicators matter?

<--- Score

90. Are the measurements objective?

<--- Score

91. What users will be impacted?

<--- Score

92. How can a multisourcing integration test verify your ideas or assumptions?

<--- Score

93. What drives O&M cost?

<--- Score

94. When a disaster occurs, who gets priority?

<--- Score

95. How do you verify multisourcing integration completeness and accuracy?

<--- Score

96. What do people want to verify?
<--- Score

97. How do your measurements capture actionable multisourcing integration information for use in exceeding your customers expectations and securing your customers engagement?
<--- Score

98. Which costs should be taken into account?
<--- Score

99. When should you bother with diagrams?
<--- Score

100. How frequently do you track multisourcing integration measures?
<--- Score

101. What are your key multisourcing integration organizational performance measures, including key short and longer-term financial measures?
<--- Score

102. Is the cost worth the multisourcing integration effort ?
<--- Score

103. How do you measure lifecycle phases?
<--- Score

104. What is the root cause(s) of the problem?
<--- Score

105. Among the multisourcing integration

product and service cost to be estimated, which is considered hardest to estimate?
<--- Score

106. How do you verify performance?
<--- Score

107. What are your operating costs?
<--- Score

108. What is the cost of rework?
<--- Score

109. How frequently do you verify your multisourcing integration strategy?
<--- Score

110. How do you verify if multisourcing integration is built right?
<--- Score

111. Do you have an issue in getting priority?
<--- Score

112. What are the operational costs after multisourcing integration deployment?
<--- Score

113. How do you aggregate measures across priorities?
<--- Score

114. Where can you go to verify the info?
<--- Score

115. What is the multisourcing integration business

impact?
<--- Score

116. What measurements are possible, practicable and meaningful?
<--- Score

117. How do you verify and validate the multisourcing integration data?
<--- Score

118. How do you verify the authenticity of the data and information used?
<--- Score

119. What causes mismanagement?
<--- Score

120. What disadvantage does this cause for the user?
<--- Score

121. How do you prevent mis-estimating cost?
<--- Score

122. Do the benefits outweigh the costs?
<--- Score

123. Which measures and indicators matter?
<--- Score

124. What would it cost to replace your technology?
<--- Score

125. What details are required of the multisourcing integration cost structure?
<--- Score

126. Are you able to realize any cost savings?
<--- Score

127. How will you measure success?
<--- Score

128. How is progress measured?
<--- Score

129. How will you measure your multisourcing integration effectiveness?
<--- Score

130. What harm might be caused?
<--- Score

131. What is the cause of any multisourcing integration gaps?
<--- Score

132. Why a multisourcing integration focus?
<--- Score

133. What does a Test Case verify?
<--- Score

134. What could cause you to change course?
<--- Score

135. What are the current costs of the multisourcing integration process?
<--- Score

136. Which multisourcing integration impacts are significant?

<--- Score

137. What are the costs and benefits?
<--- Score

138. Is there an opportunity to verify requirements?
<--- Score

Add up total points for this section:
_____ = Total points for this section

Divided by: _____ (number of
statements answered) = _____
Average score for this section

Transfer your score to the multisourcing
integration Index at the beginning of
the Self-Assessment.

CRITERION #4: ANALYZE:

INTENT: Analyze causes, assumptions and hypotheses.

In my belief, the answer to this question is clearly defined:

5 Strongly Agree

4 Agree

3 Neutral

2 Disagree

1 Strongly Disagree

1. What is the complexity of the output produced?
<--- Score

2. Who is involved with workflow mapping?
<--- Score

3. Did any additional data need to be collected?
<--- Score

4. How often will data be collected for measures?

<--- Score

5. Are multisourcing integration changes recognized early enough to be approved through the regular process?
<--- Score

6. What types of data do your multisourcing integration indicators require?
<--- Score

7. Do you, as a leader, bounce back quickly from setbacks?
<--- Score

8. What internal processes need improvement?
<--- Score

9. Can you add value to the current multisourcing integration decision-making process (largely qualitative) by incorporating uncertainty modeling (more quantitative)?
<--- Score

10. How many input/output points does it require?
<--- Score

11. How do you ensure that the multisourcing integration opportunity is realistic?
<--- Score

12. What are the processes for audit reporting and management?
<--- Score

13. What are the personnel training and qualifications

required?
<--- Score

14. How do you define collaboration and team output?
<--- Score

15. Where is the data coming from to measure compliance?
<--- Score

16. How is the way you as the leader think and process information affecting your organizational culture?
<--- Score

17. What training and qualifications will you need?
<--- Score

18. Have any additional benefits been identified that will result from closing all or most of the gaps?
<--- Score

19. Was a detailed process map created to amplify critical steps of the 'as is' stakeholder process?
<--- Score

20. What qualifications do multisourcing integration leaders need?
<--- Score

21. Did any value-added analysis or 'lean thinking' take place to identify some of the gaps shown on the 'as is' process map?
<--- Score

22. How do you promote understanding that opportunity for improvement is not criticism of the status quo, or the people who created the status quo?
<--- Score

23. How is the data gathered?
<--- Score

24. Is there an established change management process?
<--- Score

25. Identify an operational issue in your organization, for example, could a particular task be done more quickly or more efficiently by multisourcing integration?
<--- Score

26. What are the multisourcing integration design outputs?
<--- Score

27. What is the output?
<--- Score

28. Who gets your output?
<--- Score

29. What methods do you use to gather multisourcing integration data?
<--- Score

30. How is the multisourcing integration Value Stream Mapping managed?
<--- Score

31. An organizationally feasible system request is one that considers the mission, goals and objectives of the organization, key questions are: is the multisourcing integration solution request practical and will it solve a problem or take advantage of an opportunity to achieve company goals?
<--- Score

32. Do you have the authority to produce the output?
<--- Score

33. What were the financial benefits resulting from any 'ground fruit or low-hanging fruit' (quick fixes)?
<--- Score

34. Is the required multisourcing integration data gathered?
<--- Score

35. What multisourcing integration data do you gather or use now?
<--- Score

36. What output to create?
<--- Score

37. What qualifications and skills do you need?
<--- Score

38. Have you defined which data is gathered how?
<--- Score

39. What multisourcing integration metrics are outputs of the process?
<--- Score

40. What are the necessary qualifications?
<--- Score

41. How do you identify specific multisourcing integration investment opportunities and emerging trends?
<--- Score

42. Is there any way to speed up the process?
<--- Score

43. How will the change process be managed?
<--- Score

44. Which multisourcing integration data should be retained?
<--- Score

45. Do staff qualifications match your project?
<--- Score

46. A compounding model resolution with available relevant data can often provide insight towards a solution methodology; which multisourcing integration models, tools and techniques are necessary?
<--- Score

47. What conclusions were drawn from the team's data collection and analysis? How did the team reach these conclusions?
<--- Score

48. What are your current levels and trends in key multisourcing integration measures or indicators of product and process performance that are

important to and directly serve your customers?
<--- Score

49. What are the revised rough estimates of the financial savings/opportunity for multisourcing integration improvements?
<--- Score

50. Who owns what data?
<--- Score

51. What did the team gain from developing a sub-process map?
<--- Score

52. Where can you get qualified talent today?
<--- Score

53. Are gaps between current performance and the goal performance identified?
<--- Score

54. What qualifies as competition?
<--- Score

55. How difficult is it to qualify what multisourcing integration ROI is?
<--- Score

56. Who qualifies to gain access to data?
<--- Score

57. How was the detailed process map generated, verified, and validated?
<--- Score

58. What are your multisourcing integration processes?
<--- Score

59. Do quality systems drive continuous improvement?
<--- Score

60. What information qualified as important?
<--- Score

61. What are your outputs?
<--- Score

62. What are evaluation criteria for the output?
<--- Score

63. What are your current levels and trends in key measures or indicators of multisourcing integration product and process performance that are important to and directly serve your customers? How do these results compare with the performance of your competitors and other organizations with similar offerings?
<--- Score

64. How will the multisourcing integration data be captured?
<--- Score

65. What quality tools were used to get through the analyze phase?
<--- Score

66. What is your organizations process which leads to recognition of value generation?

<--- Score

67. Was a cause-and-effect diagram used to explore the different types of causes (or sources of variation)?
<--- Score

68. What tools were used to generate the list of possible causes?
<--- Score

69. Should you invest in industry-recognized qualifications?
<--- Score

70. What other organizational variables, such as reward systems or communication systems, affect the performance of this multisourcing integration process?
<--- Score

71. What is the Value Stream Mapping?
<--- Score

72. Who will gather what data?
<--- Score

73. What is the oversight process?
<--- Score

74. How do you use multisourcing integration data and information to support organizational decision making and innovation?
<--- Score

75. What tools were used to narrow the list of possible causes?

<--- Score

76. What is the multisourcing integration Driver?
<--- Score

77. What resources go in to get the desired output?
<--- Score

78. What multisourcing integration data should be managed?
<--- Score

79. Is data and process analysis, root cause analysis and quantifying the gap/opportunity in place?
<--- Score

80. Has data output been validated?
<--- Score

81. Have the problem and goal statements been updated to reflect the additional knowledge gained from the analyze phase?
<--- Score

82. Is pre-qualification of suppliers carried out?
<--- Score

83. Do your contracts/agreements contain data security obligations?
<--- Score

84. What process improvements will be needed?
<--- Score

85. How do you implement and manage your work processes to ensure that they meet design

requirements?

<--- Score

86. Is the final output clearly identified?

<--- Score

87. What are your key performance measures or indicators and in-process measures for the control and improvement of your multisourcing integration processes?

<--- Score

88. Who is involved in the management review process?

<--- Score

89. Are your outputs consistent?

<--- Score

90. What data is gathered?

<--- Score

91. Were Pareto charts (or similar) used to portray the 'heavy hitters' (or key sources of variation)?

<--- Score

92. How do mission and objectives affect the multisourcing integration processes of your organization?

<--- Score

93. What is the cost of poor quality as supported by the team's analysis?

<--- Score

94. What qualifications are needed?

<--- Score

95. What qualifications are necessary?
<--- Score

96. How much data can be collected in the given timeframe?
<--- Score

97. What were the crucial 'moments of truth' on the process map?
<--- Score

98. What do you need to qualify?
<--- Score

99. How will the data be checked for quality?
<--- Score

100. Is there a strict change management process?
<--- Score

101. What successful thing are you doing today that may be blinding you to new growth opportunities?
<--- Score

102. Think about some of the processes you undertake within your organization, which do you own?
<--- Score

103. How are outputs preserved and protected?
<--- Score

104. What does the data say about the performance

of the stakeholder process?
<--- Score

105. How do you measure the operational performance of your key work systems and processes, including productivity, cycle time, and other appropriate measures of process effectiveness, efficiency, and innovation?
<--- Score

106. Is the suppliers process defined and controlled?
<--- Score

107. What controls do you have in place to protect data?
<--- Score

108. Think about the functions involved in your multisourcing integration project, what processes flow from these functions?
<--- Score

109. Were there any improvement opportunities identified from the process analysis?
<--- Score

110. What are your best practices for minimizing multisourcing integration project risk, while demonstrating incremental value and quick wins throughout the multisourcing integration project lifecycle?
<--- Score

111. What are the disruptive multisourcing integration technologies that enable your organization to radically change your business processes?

<--- Score

112. What other jobs or tasks affect the performance of the steps in the multisourcing integration process?
<--- Score

113. Were any designed experiments used to generate additional insight into the data analysis?
<--- Score

114. How can risk management be tied procedurally to process elements?
<--- Score

115. What kind of crime could a potential new hire have committed that would not only not disqualify him/her from being hired by your organization, but would actually indicate that he/she might be a particularly good fit?
<--- Score

116. How is data used for program management and improvement?
<--- Score

117. Is the multisourcing integration process severely broken such that a re-design is necessary?
<--- Score

118. What multisourcing integration data should be collected?
<--- Score

119. Is the performance gap determined?
<--- Score

120. Are all team members qualified for all tasks?
<--- Score

121. Do your employees have the opportunity to do what they do best everyday?
<--- Score

122. Are you missing multisourcing integration opportunities?
<--- Score

123. Is the gap/opportunity displayed and communicated in financial terms?
<--- Score

124. How has the multisourcing integration data been gathered?
<--- Score

125. What will drive multisourcing integration change?
<--- Score

126. What, related to, multisourcing integration processes does your organization outsource?
<--- Score

127. Do your leaders quickly bounce back from setbacks?
<--- Score

128. Are all staff in core multisourcing integration subjects Highly Qualified?
<--- Score

129. Record-keeping requirements flow from the records needed as inputs, outputs, controls and for transformation of a multisourcing integration process, are the records needed as inputs to the multisourcing integration process available?
<--- Score

130. What are the multisourcing integration business drivers?
<--- Score

131. Has an output goal been set?
<--- Score

132. How will corresponding data be collected?
<--- Score

133. What multisourcing integration data will be collected?
<--- Score

134. What systems/processes must you excel at?
<--- Score

135. Do several people in different organizational units assist with the multisourcing integration process?
<--- Score

136. What data do you need to collect?
<--- Score

Add up total points for this section:
_ _ _ _ _ = Total points for this section

Divided by: _ _ _ _ _ _ (number of

statements answered) = _____
Average score for this section

Transfer your score to the multisourcing
integration Index at the beginning of
the Self-Assessment.

CRITERION #5: IMPROVE:

INTENT: Develop a practical solution. Innovate, establish and test the solution and to measure the results.

In my belief, the answer to this question is clearly defined:

5 Strongly Agree

4 Agree

3 Neutral

2 Disagree

1 Strongly Disagree

1. Which multisourcing integration solution is appropriate?
<--- Score

2. What can you do to improve?
<--- Score

3. Can you identify any significant risks or exposures to multisourcing integration third- parties (vendors,

service providers, alliance partners etc) that concern you?
<--- Score

4. How do the multisourcing integration results compare with the performance of your competitors and other organizations with similar offerings?
<--- Score

5. What resources are required for the improvement efforts?
<--- Score

6. How do you keep improving multisourcing integration?
<--- Score

7. How significant is the improvement in the eyes of the end user?
<--- Score

8. Is there a high likelihood that any recommendations will achieve their intended results?
<--- Score

9. What multisourcing integration improvements can be made?
<--- Score

10. In the past few months, what is the smallest change you have made that has had the biggest positive result? What was it about that small change that produced the large return?
<--- Score

11. How scalable is your multisourcing integration

solution?
<--- Score

12. Who manages multisourcing integration risk?
<--- Score

13. Do you cover the five essential competencies:
Communication, Collaboration,Innovation,
Adaptability, and Leadership that improve
an organizations ability to leverage the new
multisourcing integration in a volatile global
economy?
<--- Score

14. Do you need to do a usability evaluation?
<--- Score

15. What is the risk?
<--- Score

16. Are the most efficient solutions problem-specific?
<--- Score

17. Risk Identification: What are the possible
risk events your organization faces in relation to
multisourcing integration?
<--- Score

**18. Do vendor agreements bring new compliance
risk ?**
<--- Score

19. Is risk periodically assessed?
<--- Score

20. Do those selected for the multisourcing

integration team have a good general understanding of what multisourcing integration is all about?

<--- Score

21. Who are the people involved in developing and implementing multisourcing integration?

<--- Score

22. Where do you need multisourcing integration improvement?

<--- Score

23. How do you manage and improve your multisourcing integration work systems to deliver customer value and achieve organizational success and sustainability?

<--- Score

24. Can the solution be designed and implemented within an acceptable time period?

<--- Score

25. What is the magnitude of the improvements?

<--- Score

26. How will you recognize and celebrate results?

<--- Score

27. Who will be responsible for making the decisions to include or exclude requested changes once multisourcing integration is underway?

<--- Score

28. What area needs the greatest improvement?

<--- Score

29. What needs improvement? Why?
<--- Score

30. What is the multisourcing integration's sustainability risk?
<--- Score

31. How does your organization evaluate strategic multisourcing integration success?
<--- Score

32. How is knowledge sharing about risk management improved?
<--- Score

33. How risky is your organization?
<--- Score

34. Is the solution technically practical?
<--- Score

35. Who should make the multisourcing integration decisions?
<--- Score

36. What should a proof of concept or pilot accomplish?
<--- Score

37. How do you define the solutions' scope?
<--- Score

38. Does the goal represent a desired result that can be measured?
<--- Score

39. Have you identified breakpoints and/or risk tolerances that will trigger broad consideration of a potential need for intervention or modification of strategy?
<--- Score

40. Was a multisourcing integration charter developed?
<--- Score

41. Are decisions made in a timely manner?
<--- Score

42. What current systems have to be understood and/or changed?
<--- Score

43. What is multisourcing integration risk?
<--- Score

44. Is the multisourcing integration risk managed?
<--- Score

45. What is the team's contingency plan for potential problems occurring in implementation?
<--- Score

46. How will you know that you have improved?
<--- Score

47. Are the key business and technology risks being managed?
<--- Score

48. What tools were used to tap into the creativity and

encourage 'outside the box' thinking?
<--- Score

49. Have you achieved multisourcing integration improvements?
<--- Score

50. How can you better manage risk?
<--- Score

51. What were the underlying assumptions on the cost-benefit analysis?
<--- Score

52. Is the multisourcing integration solution sustainable?
<--- Score

53. Is the scope clearly documented?
<--- Score

54. Are the risks fully understood, reasonable and manageable?
<--- Score

55. What tools were most useful during the improve phase?
<--- Score

56. Is supporting multisourcing integration documentation required?
<--- Score

57. How can you improve multisourcing integration?
<--- Score

58. What risks do you need to manage?
<--- Score

59. How will you measure the results?
<--- Score

60. How do you decide how much to remunerate an employee?
<--- Score

61. Who makes the multisourcing integration decisions in your organization?
<--- Score

62. At what point will vulnerability assessments be performed once multisourcing integration is put into production (e.g., ongoing Risk Management after implementation)?
<--- Score

63. Is the multisourcing integration documentation thorough?
<--- Score

64. How do you improve multisourcing integration service perception, and satisfaction?
<--- Score

65. Who are the multisourcing integration decision makers?
<--- Score

66. multisourcing integration risk decisions: whose call Is It?
<--- Score

67. What actually has to improve and by how much?

<--- Score

68. Who do you report multisourcing integration results to?

<--- Score

69. Risk factors: what are the characteristics of multisourcing integration that make it risky?

<--- Score

70. How do you measure improved multisourcing integration service perception, and satisfaction?

<--- Score

71. Does a good decision guarantee a good outcome?

<--- Score

72. When you map the key players in your own work and the types/domains of relationships with them, which relationships do you find easy and which challenging, and why?

<--- Score

73. What were the criteria for evaluating a multisourcing integration pilot?

<--- Score

74. How do you deal with multisourcing integration risk?

<--- Score

75. Why improve in the first place?

<--- Score

76. For estimation problems, how do you develop an estimation statement?
<--- Score

77. How do you improve your likelihood of success ?
<--- Score

78. Are procedures documented for managing multisourcing integration risks?
<--- Score

79. For decision problems, how do you develop a decision statement?
<--- Score

80. How do you mitigate multisourcing integration risk?
<--- Score

81. What to do with the results or outcomes of measurements?
<--- Score

82. How are policy decisions made and where?
<--- Score

83. Who are the key stakeholders for the multisourcing integration evaluation?
<--- Score

84. What assumptions are made about the solution and approach?
<--- Score

85. What is multisourcing integration's impact on

utilizing the best solution(s)?
<--- Score

86. What are the concrete multisourcing integration results?
<--- Score

87. Is multisourcing integration documentation maintained?
<--- Score

88. What tools were used to evaluate the potential solutions?
<--- Score

89. What are the affordable multisourcing integration risks?
<--- Score

90. Who will be using the results of the measurement activities?
<--- Score

91. Where do the multisourcing integration decisions reside?
<--- Score

92. How do you improve productivity?
<--- Score

93. How do you measure risk?
<--- Score

94. If you could go back in time five years, what decision would you make differently? What is your best guess as to what decision you're making today

you might regret five years from now?
<--- Score

95. What are your current levels and trends in key measures or indicators of workforce and leader development?
<--- Score

96. Who will be responsible for documenting the multisourcing integration requirements in detail?
<--- Score

97. What are the implications of the one critical multisourcing integration decision 10 minutes, 10 months, and 10 years from now?
<--- Score

98. Do you have the optimal project management team structure?
<--- Score

99. What alternative responses are available to manage risk?
<--- Score

100. To what extent does management recognize multisourcing integration as a tool to increase the results?
<--- Score

101. What lessons, if any, from a pilot were incorporated into the design of the full-scale solution?
<--- Score

102. How will you know when its improved?
<--- Score

103. Explorations of the frontiers of multisourcing integration will help you build influence, improve multisourcing integration, optimize decision making, and sustain change, what is your approach?
<--- Score

104. What went well, what should change, what can improve?
<--- Score

105. Is there any other multisourcing integration solution?
<--- Score

106. Which of the recognised risks out of all risks can be most likely transferred?
<--- Score

107. Are you assessing multisourcing integration and risk?
<--- Score

108. How do you manage multisourcing integration risk?
<--- Score

109. Are events managed to resolution?
<--- Score

110. How do you measure progress and evaluate training effectiveness?
<--- Score

111. Are risk triggers captured?
<--- Score

112. How will you know that a change is an improvement?

<--- Score

113. Who do you report multisourcing integration results to?

<--- Score

114. How can you improve performance?

<--- Score

115. Can you integrate quality management and risk management?

<--- Score

116. Who are the multisourcing integration decision-makers?

<--- Score

117. How are multisourcing integration risks managed?

<--- Score

118. What tools do you use once you have decided on a multisourcing integration strategy and more importantly how do you choose?

<--- Score

119. Risk events: what are the things that could go wrong?

<--- Score

120. What are the multisourcing integration security risks?

<--- Score

121. How do you link measurement and risk?
<--- Score

122. How do you go about comparing multisourcing integration approaches/solutions?
<--- Score

123. What strategies for multisourcing integration improvement are successful?
<--- Score

124. Will the controls trigger any other risks?
<--- Score

125. What do you want to improve?
<--- Score

126. How is continuous improvement applied to risk management?
<--- Score

127. Is any multisourcing integration documentation required?
<--- Score

128. How does the team improve its work?
<--- Score

129. Would you develop a multisourcing integration Communication Strategy?
<--- Score

130. What are the expected multisourcing integration results?
<--- Score

Add up total points for this section:
_____ = Total points for this section

Divided by: _____ (number of
statements answered) = _____
Average score for this section

Transfer your score to the multisourcing
integration Index at the beginning of
the Self-Assessment.

CRITERION #6: CONTROL:

INTENT: Implement the practical solution. Maintain the performance and correct possible complications.

In my belief, the answer to this question is clearly defined:

5 Strongly Agree

4 Agree

3 Neutral

2 Disagree

1 Strongly Disagree

1. Is a response plan in place for when the input, process, or output measures indicate an 'out-of-control' condition?
<--- Score

2. What do you stand for--and what are you against?
<--- Score

3. Does job training on the documented procedures

need to be part of the process team's education and training?

<--- Score

4. Is there a standardized process?

<--- Score

5. How do you select, collect, align, and integrate multisourcing integration data and information for tracking daily operations and overall organizational performance, including progress relative to strategic objectives and action plans?

<--- Score

6. Are suggested corrective/restorative actions indicated on the response plan for known causes to problems that might surface?

<--- Score

7. Is reporting being used or needed?

<--- Score

8. How is change control managed?

<--- Score

9. What is the recommended frequency of auditing?

<--- Score

10. Is there a recommended audit plan for routine surveillance inspections of multisourcing integration's gains?

<--- Score

11. Are there documented procedures?

<--- Score

12. Is the multisourcing integration test/monitoring cost justified?
<--- Score

13. What do you measure to verify effectiveness gains?
<--- Score

14. Who sets the multisourcing integration standards?
<--- Score

15. Can support from partners be adjusted?
<--- Score

16. What adjustments to the strategies are needed?
<--- Score

17. What are the key elements of your multisourcing integration performance improvement system, including your evaluation, organizational learning, and innovation processes?
<--- Score

18. What key inputs and outputs are being measured on an ongoing basis?
<--- Score

19. What are the performance and scale of the multisourcing integration tools?
<--- Score

20. Who controls critical resources?
<--- Score

21. Is a response plan established and deployed?
<--- Score

22. Is there a transfer of ownership and knowledge to process owner and process team tasked with the responsibilities.
<--- Score

23. Are controls in place and consistently applied?
<--- Score

24. How do controls support value?
<--- Score

25. What can you control?
<--- Score

26. Will the team be available to assist members in planning investigations?
<--- Score

27. Against what alternative is success being measured?
<--- Score

28. Are operating procedures consistent?
<--- Score

29. Is there a multisourcing integration Communication plan covering who needs to get what information when?
<--- Score

30. How widespread is its use?
<--- Score

31. Does the response plan contain a definite closed loop continual improvement scheme (e.g., plan-do-check-act)?
<--- Score

32. Are the planned controls in place?
<--- Score

33. Have new or revised work instructions resulted?
<--- Score

34. Will any special training be provided for results interpretation?
<--- Score

35. What is your theory of human motivation, and how does your compensation plan fit with that view?
<--- Score

36. How is multisourcing integration project cost planned, managed, monitored?
<--- Score

37. In the case of a multisourcing integration project, the criteria for the audit derive from implementation objectives, an audit of a multisourcing integration project involves assessing whether the recommendations outlined for implementation have been met, can you track that any multisourcing integration project is implemented as planned, and is it working?
<--- Score

38. Do the viable solutions scale to future needs?
<--- Score

39. How do your controls stack up?
<--- Score

40. Is there a control plan in place for sustaining improvements (short and long-term)?
<--- Score

41. What should you measure to verify efficiency gains?
<--- Score

42. What quality tools were useful in the control phase?
<--- Score

43. What do your reports reflect?
<--- Score

44. What are the known security controls?
<--- Score

45. How will multisourcing integration decisions be made and monitored?
<--- Score

46. Does a troubleshooting guide exist or is it needed?
<--- Score

47. Does multisourcing integration appropriately measure and monitor risk?
<--- Score

48. What is the best design framework for multisourcing integration organization now that, in a post industrial-age if the top-down, command

and control model is no longer relevant?
<--- Score

49. How might the group capture best practices and lessons learned so as to leverage improvements?
<--- Score

50. What is your plan to assess your security risks?
<--- Score

51. Are the planned controls working?
<--- Score

52. Are new process steps, standards, and documentation ingrained into normal operations?
<--- Score

53. Will existing staff require re-training, for example, to learn new business processes?
<--- Score

54. Is there a documented and implemented monitoring plan?
<--- Score

55. What multisourcing integration standards are applicable?
<--- Score

56. Is new knowledge gained imbedded in the response plan?
<--- Score

57. Who is the multisourcing integration process owner?
<--- Score

58. Do you monitor the effectiveness of your multisourcing integration activities?
<--- Score

59. How do you encourage people to take control and responsibility?
<--- Score

60. How do you plan for the cost of succession?
<--- Score

61. Who is going to spread your message?
<--- Score

62. How will input, process, and output variables be checked to detect for sub-optimal conditions?
<--- Score

63. What should the next improvement project be that is related to multisourcing integration?
<--- Score

64. What other systems, operations, processes, and infrastructures (hiring practices, staffing, training, incentives/rewards, metrics/dashboards/scorecards, etc.) need updates, additions, changes, or deletions in order to facilitate knowledge transfer and improvements?
<--- Score

65. Where do ideas that reach policy makers and planners as proposals for multisourcing integration strengthening and reform actually originate?
<--- Score

66. Are documented procedures clear and easy to follow for the operators?
<--- Score

67. Is knowledge gained on process shared and institutionalized?
<--- Score

68. How will the day-to-day responsibilities for monitoring and continual improvement be transferred from the improvement team to the process owner?
<--- Score

69. What other areas of the group might benefit from the multisourcing integration team's improvements, knowledge, and learning?
<--- Score

70. How do senior leaders actions reflect a commitment to the organizations multisourcing integration values?
<--- Score

71. You may have created your quality measures at a time when you lacked resources, technology wasn't up to the required standard, or low service levels were the industry norm. Have those circumstances changed?
<--- Score

72. Act/Adjust: What Do you Need to Do Differently?
<--- Score

73. Are pertinent alerts monitored, analyzed and

distributed to appropriate personnel?
<--- Score

74. What are your results for key measures or indicators of the accomplishment of your multisourcing integration strategy and action plans, including building and strengthening core competencies?
<--- Score

75. How can you best use all of your knowledge repositories to enhance learning and sharing?
<--- Score

76. How will you measure your QA plan's effectiveness?
<--- Score

77. Is there documentation that will support the successful operation of the improvement?
<--- Score

78. Is there an action plan in case of emergencies?
<--- Score

79. What are the critical parameters to watch?
<--- Score

80. Who will be in control?
<--- Score

81. Do the multisourcing integration decisions you make today help people and the planet tomorrow?
<--- Score

82. Has the improved process and its steps been

standardized?
<--- Score

83. How will report readings be checked to effectively monitor performance?
<--- Score

84. Will your goals reflect your program budget?
<--- Score

85. How do you establish and deploy modified action plans if circumstances require a shift in plans and rapid execution of new plans?
<--- Score

86. Who has control over resources?
<--- Score

87. What are customers monitoring?
<--- Score

88. How will the process owner and team be able to hold the gains?
<--- Score

89. How will the process owner verify improvement in present and future sigma levels, process capabilities?
<--- Score

90. How will new or emerging customer needs/requirements be checked/communicated to orient the process toward meeting the new specifications and continually reducing variation?
<--- Score

91. What is the standard for acceptable multisourcing

integration performance?

<--- Score

92. How likely is the current multisourcing integration plan to come in on schedule or on budget?

<--- Score

93. Does the multisourcing integration performance meet the customer's requirements?

<--- Score

94. Can you adapt and adjust to changing multisourcing integration situations?

<--- Score

95. What is the control/monitoring plan?

<--- Score

Add up total points for this section:

_ _ _ _ _ = Total points for this section

Divided by: _ _ _ _ _ _ (number of statements answered) = _ _ _ _ _ _
Average score for this section

Transfer your score to the multisourcing integration Index at the beginning of the Self-Assessment.

CRITERION #7: SUSTAIN:

INTENT: Retain the benefits.

In my belief, the answer to this
question is clearly defined:

5 Strongly Agree

4 Agree

3 Neutral

2 Disagree

1 Strongly Disagree

**1. Who, on the executive team or the board, has
spoken to a customer recently?**
<--- Score

2. How do you know if you are successful?
<--- Score

3. How important is multisourcing integration to the
user organizations mission?
<--- Score

4. Are your responses positive or negative?
<--- Score

5. Are you relevant? Will you be relevant five years from now? Ten?
<--- Score

6. Do you think you know, or do you know you know ?
<--- Score

7. Why is it important to have senior management support for a multisourcing integration project?
<--- Score

8. Is multisourcing integration realistic, or are you setting yourself up for failure?
<--- Score

9. When information truly is ubiquitous, when reach and connectivity are completely global, when computing resources are infinite, and when a whole new set of impossibilities are not only possible, but happening, what will that do to your business?
<--- Score

10. How do you assess the multisourcing integration pitfalls that are inherent in implementing it?
<--- Score

11. Is there any reason to believe the opposite of my current belief?
<--- Score

12. What is the purpose of multisourcing integration in relation to the mission?

<--- Score

13. What do we do when new problems arise?
<--- Score

14. If there were zero limitations, what would you do differently?
<--- Score

15. What is the range of capabilities?
<--- Score

16. What are current multisourcing integration paradigms?
<--- Score

17. What could happen if you do not do it?
<--- Score

18. What are the top 3 things at the forefront of your multisourcing integration agendas for the next 3 years?
<--- Score

19. Are you maintaining a past–present–future perspective throughout the multisourcing integration discussion?
<--- Score

20. What is the overall talent health of your organization as a whole at senior levels, and for each organization reporting to a member of the Senior Leadership Team?
<--- Score

21. Who do you think the world wants your

organization to be?
<--- Score

22. What would you recommend your friend do if he/she were facing this dilemma?
<--- Score

23. Do you have the right capabilities and capacities?
<--- Score

24. What are the gaps in your knowledge and experience?
<--- Score

25. Who is responsible for errors?
<--- Score

26. Are there any activities that you can take off your to do list?
<--- Score

27. What management system can you use to leverage the multisourcing integration experience, ideas, and concerns of the people closest to the work to be done?
<--- Score

28. How do you keep records, of what?
<--- Score

29. Who do you want your customers to become?
<--- Score

30. What is the funding source for this project?
<--- Score

31. Why is multisourcing integration important for you now?
<--- Score

32. If you weren't already in this business, would you enter it today? And if not, what are you going to do about it?
<--- Score

33. What happens when a new employee joins the organization?
<--- Score

34. What are your most important goals for the strategic multisourcing integration objectives?
<--- Score

35. Who are the key stakeholders?
<--- Score

36. What are the usability implications of multisourcing integration actions?
<--- Score

37. What trophy do you want on your mantle?
<--- Score

38. Which models, tools and techniques are necessary?
<--- Score

39. What is something you believe that nearly no one agrees with you on?
<--- Score

40. What did you miss in the interview for the

worst hire you ever made?
<--- Score

41. What is a feasible sequencing of reform initiatives over time?
<--- Score

42. How are you doing compared to your industry?
<--- Score

43. What is an unauthorized commitment?
<--- Score

44. What is your question? Why?
<--- Score

45. What is it like to work for you?
<--- Score

46. If you got fired and a new hire took your place, what would she do different?
<--- Score

47. If you do not follow, then how to lead?
<--- Score

48. Why should people listen to you?
<--- Score

49. In the past year, what have you done (or could you have done) to increase the accurate perception of your company/brand as ethical and honest?
<--- Score

50. Is a multisourcing integration team work effort in

place?
<--- Score

51. How will you motivate the stakeholders with the least vested interest?
<--- Score

52. What are you challenging?
<--- Score

53. Who is responsible for ensuring appropriate resources (time, people and money) are allocated to multisourcing integration?
<--- Score

54. Do multisourcing integration rules make a reasonable demand on a users capabilities?
<--- Score

55. What may be the consequences for the performance of an organization if all stakeholders are not consulted regarding multisourcing integration?
<--- Score

56. What does your signature ensure?
<--- Score

57. If your customer were your grandmother, would you tell her to buy what you're selling?
<--- Score

58. What is your formula for success in multisourcing integration ?
<--- Score

59. Are you using a design thinking approach and

integrating Innovation, multisourcing integration Experience, and Brand Value?
<--- Score

60. How will you insure seamless interoperability of multisourcing integration moving forward?
<--- Score

61. What you are going to do to affect the numbers?
<--- Score

62. What are the success criteria that will indicate that multisourcing integration objectives have been met and the benefits delivered?
<--- Score

63. Whose voice (department, ethnic group, women, older workers, etc) might you have missed hearing from in your company, and how might you amplify this voice to create positive momentum for your business?
<--- Score

64. What must you excel at?
<--- Score

65. Political -is anyone trying to undermine this project?
<--- Score

66. What are the business goals multisourcing integration is aiming to achieve?
<--- Score

67. Are you paying enough attention to the partners your company depends on to succeed?

<--- Score

68. If your company went out of business tomorrow, would anyone who doesn't get a paycheck here care?
<--- Score

69. How can you become the company that would put you out of business?
<--- Score

70. At what moment would you think; Will I get fired?
<--- Score

71. What is the source of the strategies for multisourcing integration strengthening and reform?
<--- Score

72. How do you transition from the baseline to the target?
<--- Score

73. How much contingency will be available in the budget?
<--- Score

74. How can you become more high-tech but still be high touch?
<--- Score

75. What are the long-term multisourcing integration goals?
<--- Score

76. To whom do you add value?
<--- Score

77. Are assumptions made in multisourcing integration stated explicitly?
<--- Score

78. Instead of going to current contacts for new ideas, what if you reconnected with dormant contacts--the people you used to know? If you were going reactivate a dormant tie, who would it be?
<--- Score

79. Is the multisourcing integration organization completing tasks effectively and efficiently?
<--- Score

80. Do you feel that more should be done in the multisourcing integration area?
<--- Score

81. Whom among your colleagues do you trust, and for what?
<--- Score

82. How do you go about securing multisourcing integration?
<--- Score

83. What new services of functionality will be implemented next with multisourcing integration ?
<--- Score

84. What are the barriers to increased multisourcing integration production?
<--- Score

85. Is it economical; do you have the time and money?

<--- Score

86. If you had to leave your organization for a year and the only communication you could have with employees/colleagues was a single paragraph, what would you write?

<--- Score

87. How do you engage the workforce, in addition to satisfying them?

<--- Score

88. How do customers see your organization?

<--- Score

89. Why not do multisourcing integration?

<--- Score

90. Is there any existing multisourcing integration governance structure?

<--- Score

91. If you find that you havent accomplished one of the goals for one of the steps of the multisourcing integration strategy, what will you do to fix it?

<--- Score

92. How do you cross-sell and up-sell your multisourcing integration success?

<--- Score

93. How do you lead with multisourcing integration in mind?

<--- Score

94. Is your basic point _____ or _____?
<--- Score

95. What are the challenges?
<--- Score

96. What was the last experiment you ran?
<--- Score

97. Do you say no to customers for no reason?
<--- Score

98. How will you ensure you get what you expected?
<--- Score

99. Think of your multisourcing integration project, what are the main functions?
<--- Score

100. Is there a work around that you can use?
<--- Score

101. Who will be responsible for deciding whether multisourcing integration goes ahead or not after the initial investigations?
<--- Score

102. Can you maintain your growth without detracting from the factors that have contributed to your success?
<--- Score

103. What role does communication play in the

success or failure of a multisourcing integration project?
<--- Score

104. If no one would ever find out about your accomplishments, how would you lead differently?
<--- Score

105. Ask yourself: how would you do this work if you only had one staff member to do it?
<--- Score

106. Can you break it down?
<--- Score

107. What is your multisourcing integration strategy?
<--- Score

108. How do you listen to customers to obtain actionable information?
<--- Score

109. Where can you break convention?
<--- Score

110. How can you negotiate multisourcing integration successfully with a stubborn boss, an irate client, or a deceitful coworker?
<--- Score

111. Do you know what you are doing? And who do you call if you don't?
<--- Score

112. Is maximizing multisourcing integration protection the same as minimizing multisourcing

integration loss?

<--- Score

113. What threat is multisourcing integration addressing?

<--- Score

114. How do you deal with multisourcing integration changes?

<--- Score

115. What goals did you miss?

<--- Score

116. What relationships among multisourcing integration trends do you perceive?

<--- Score

117. Do you think multisourcing integration accomplishes the goals you expect it to accomplish?

<--- Score

118. How do you foster the skills, knowledge, talents, attributes, and characteristics you want to have?

<--- Score

119. Who is responsible for multisourcing integration?

<--- Score

120. Are the assumptions believable and achievable?

<--- Score

121. Who is the main stakeholder, with ultimate responsibility for driving multisourcing integration forward?

<--- Score

122. What have you done to protect your business from competitive encroachment?
<--- Score

123. Who will provide the final approval of multisourcing integration deliverables?
<--- Score

124. Is multisourcing integration dependent on the successful delivery of a current project?
<--- Score

125. Are the criteria for selecting recommendations stated?
<--- Score

126. Who will manage the integration of tools?
<--- Score

127. How do you set multisourcing integration stretch targets and how do you get people to not only participate in setting these stretch targets but also that they strive to achieve these?
<--- Score

128. What unique value proposition (UVP) do you offer?
<--- Score

129. What multisourcing integration skills are most important?
<--- Score

130. Are you changing as fast as the world around you?

<--- Score

131. What multisourcing integration modifications can you make work for you?
<--- Score

132. What have been your experiences in defining long range multisourcing integration goals?
<--- Score

133. How do you make it meaningful in connecting multisourcing integration with what users do day-to-day?
<--- Score

134. Which individuals, teams or departments will be involved in multisourcing integration?
<--- Score

135. Who is on the team?
<--- Score

136. What are the key enablers to make this multisourcing integration move?
<--- Score

137. What information is critical to your organization that your executives are ignoring?
<--- Score

138. What are you trying to prove to yourself, and how might it be hijacking your life and business success?
<--- Score

139. What are your personal philosophies regarding multisourcing integration and how do they influence

your work?
<--- Score

140. What is the kind of project structure that would be appropriate for your multisourcing integration project, should it be formal and complex, or can it be less formal and relatively simple?
<--- Score

141. What are internal and external multisourcing integration relations?
<--- Score

142. What is the big multisourcing integration idea?
<--- Score

143. Which functions and people interact with the supplier and or customer?
<--- Score

144. Why do and why don't your customers like your organization?
<--- Score

145. How does multisourcing integration integrate with other stakeholder initiatives?
<--- Score

146. Is your strategy driving your strategy? Or is the way in which you allocate resources driving your strategy?
<--- Score

147. What are the essentials of internal multisourcing integration management?
<--- Score

148. Operational - will it work?
<--- Score

149. Do you have the right people on the bus?
<--- Score

150. What business benefits will multisourcing integration goals deliver if achieved?
<--- Score

151. How will you know that the multisourcing integration project has been successful?
<--- Score

152. What are the short and long-term multisourcing integration goals?
<--- Score

153. Have benefits been optimized with all key stakeholders?
<--- Score

154. How do you manage multisourcing integration Knowledge Management (KM)?
<--- Score

155. Are new benefits received and understood?
<--- Score

156. Who are four people whose careers you have enhanced?
<--- Score

157. Will it be accepted by users?
<--- Score

158. What potential megatrends could make your business model obsolete?
<--- Score

159. Who are your customers?
<--- Score

160. How long will it take to change?
<--- Score

161. What happens if you do not have enough funding?
<--- Score

162. Will there be any necessary staff changes (redundancies or new hires)?
<--- Score

163. Do you have an implicit bias for capital investments over people investments?
<--- Score

164. In a project to restructure multisourcing integration outcomes, which stakeholders would you involve?
<--- Score

165. How is implementation research currently incorporated into each of your goals?
<--- Score

166. What counts that you are not counting?
<--- Score

167. What would have to be true for the option on the

table to be the best possible choice?
<--- Score

168. What are strategies for increasing support and reducing opposition?
<--- Score

169. How do you keep the momentum going?
<--- Score

170. Has implementation been effective in reaching specified objectives so far?
<--- Score

171. Who uses your product in ways you never expected?
<--- Score

172. Do you have past multisourcing integration successes?
<--- Score

173. How do you accomplish your long range multisourcing integration goals?
<--- Score

174. How do you ensure that implementations of multisourcing integration products are done in a way that ensures safety?
<--- Score

175. How do you determine the key elements that affect multisourcing integration workforce satisfaction, how are these elements determined for different workforce groups and segments?
<--- Score

176. How do you stay inspired?
<--- Score

177. What is the recommended frequency of auditing?
<--- Score

178. What trouble can you get into?
<--- Score

179. How can you incorporate support to ensure safe and effective use of multisourcing integration into the services that you provide?
<--- Score

180. What are the potential basics of multisourcing integration fraud?
<--- Score

181. Who will determine interim and final deadlines?
<--- Score

182. Can you do all this work?
<--- Score

183. Do you know who is a friend or a foe?
<--- Score

184. Would you rather sell to knowledgeable and informed customers or to uninformed customers?
<--- Score

185. Are you making progress, and are you making progress as multisourcing integration leaders?
<--- Score

186. In retrospect, of the projects that you pulled the plug on, what percent do you wish had been allowed to keep going, and what percent do you wish had ended earlier?
<--- Score

187. How do senior leaders deploy your organizations vision and values through your leadership system, to the workforce, to key suppliers and partners, and to customers and other stakeholders, as appropriate?
<--- Score

188. Why should you adopt a multisourcing integration framework?
<--- Score

189. How do you govern and fulfill your societal responsibilities?
<--- Score

190. Is a multisourcing integration breakthrough on the horizon?
<--- Score

191. How do you create buy-in?
<--- Score

192. What should you stop doing?
<--- Score

193. What is your competitive advantage?
<--- Score

194. Do you see more potential in people than they do in themselves?
<--- Score

195. What is the craziest thing you can do?
<--- Score

196. What knowledge, skills and characteristics mark a good multisourcing integration project manager?
<--- Score

197. How do you provide a safe environment -physically and emotionally?
<--- Score

198. Can the schedule be done in the given time?
<--- Score

199. How do you maintain multisourcing integration's Integrity?
<--- Score

200. Were lessons learned captured and communicated?
<--- Score

201. Are you satisfied with your current role? If not, what is missing from it?
<--- Score

202. Who do we want your customers to become?
<--- Score

203. What is your BATNA (best alternative to a negotiated agreement)?
<--- Score

204. Do you have enough freaky customers in your portfolio pushing you to the limit day in and day out?

<--- Score

205. Who else should you help?
<--- Score

206. How do you proactively clarify deliverables and multisourcing integration quality expectations?
<--- Score

207. Who have you, as a company, historically been when you've been at your best?
<--- Score

208. How do you foster innovation?
<--- Score

209. Is the impact that multisourcing integration has shown?
<--- Score

210. How likely is it that a customer would recommend your company to a friend or colleague?
<--- Score

211. What are specific multisourcing integration rules to follow?
<--- Score

212. Did your employees make progress today?
<--- Score

213. Which multisourcing integration goals are the most important?
<--- Score

214. How much does multisourcing integration help?

<--- Score

215. Have new benefits been realized?

<--- Score

216. What is the overall business strategy?

<--- Score

217. What happens at your organization when people fail?

<--- Score

Add up total points for this section:
_ _ _ _ _ = Total points for this section

Divided by: _ _ _ _ _ _ (number of statements answered) = _ _ _ _ _ _
Average score for this section

Transfer your score to the multisourcing integration Index at the beginning of the Self-Assessment.

Multisourcing Integration and Managing Projects, Criteria for Project Managers:

1.0 Initiating Process Group: Multisourcing Integration

1. If the risk event occurs, what will you do?

2. Professionals want to know what is expected from them what are the deliverables?

3. How to control and approve each phase?

4. Were resources available as planned?

5. How will it affect me?

6. How well did the chosen processes produce the expected results?

7. Mitigate. what will you do to minimize the impact should the risk event occur?

8. What is the NEXT thing to do?

9. Are the Multisourcing Integration project team and stakeholders meeting regularly and using a meeting agenda and taking notes to accurately document what is being covered and what happened in the weekly meetings?

10. Were decisions made in a timely manner?

11. How is each deliverable reviewed, verified, and validated?

12. Which of six sigmas dmaic phases focuses on the measurement of internal process that affect factors

that are critical to quality?

13. What input will you be required to provide the Multisourcing Integration project team?

14. How will you do it?

15. Do you know if the Multisourcing Integration project requires outside equipment or vendor resources?

16. Did you use a contractor or vendor?

17. What communication items need improvement?

18. How should needs be met?

19. Who is funding the Multisourcing Integration project?

1.1 Project Charter: Multisourcing Integration

20. What are the constraints?

21. What barriers do you predict to your success?

22. What are some examples of a business case?

23. Where and how does the team fit within your organization structure?

24. When is a charter needed?

25. Avoid costs, improve service, and/ or comply with a mandate?

26. Fit with other Products Compliments – Cannibalizes?

27. Does the Multisourcing Integration project need to consider any special capacity or capability issues?

28. Who will take notes, document decisions?

29. Why do you manage integration?

30. Assumptions and constraints: what assumptions were made in defining the Multisourcing Integration project?

31. Why is a Multisourcing Integration project Charter used?

32. Why have you chosen the aim you have set forth?

33. What outcome, in measureable terms, are you hoping to accomplish?

34. What is the justification?

35. Why use a Multisourcing Integration project charter?

36. What is the business need?

37. Why Outsource?

38. What are the deliverables?

39. What ideas do you have for initial tests of change (PDSA cycles)?

1.2 Stakeholder Register: Multisourcing Integration

40. Who wants to talk about Security?

41. What is the power of the stakeholder?

42. What are the major Multisourcing Integration project milestones requiring communications or providing communications opportunities?

43. Is your organization ready for change?

44. What opportunities exist to provide communications?

45. Who are the stakeholders?

46. What & Why?

47. How should employers make voices heard?

48. How big is the gap?

49. How will reports be created?

50. Who is managing stakeholder engagement?

51. How much influence do they have on the Multisourcing Integration project?

1.3 Stakeholder Analysis Matrix: Multisourcing Integration

52. How to involve media?

53. What is the stakeholders power and status in relation to the Multisourcing Integration project?

54. How do rules, behaviors affect stakes?

55. What are the reimbursement requirements?

56. What is the stakeholders name, what is function?

57. Who can contribute financial or technical resources towards the work?

58. Organizational Applicability?

59. Identify the stakeholders levels most frequently used –or at least sought– in your Multisourcing Integration projects and for which purpose?

60. Market demand?

61. How are you predicting what future (work)loads will be?

62. Competitors vulnerabilities?

63. Advantages of proposition?

64. Contributions to policy and practice?

65. Supporters; who are the supporters?

66. Who will obstruct/hinder the Multisourcing Integration project if they are not involved?

67. Who will be affected by the work?

68. Location and geographical?

69. What do you Evaluate?

70. Who are potential allies and opponents?

71. How do customers express needs?

2.0 Planning Process Group: Multisourcing Integration

72. To what extent are the visions and actions of the partners consistent or divergent with regard to the program?

73. Are the follow-up indicators relevant and do they meet the quality needed to measure the outputs and outcomes of the Multisourcing Integration project?

74. To what extent do the intervention objectives and strategies of the Multisourcing Integration project respond to your organizations plans?

75. What makes your Multisourcing Integration project successful?

76. What is the difference between the early schedule and late schedule?

77. Are the necessary foundations in place to ensure the sustainability of the results of the Multisourcing Integration project?

78. What is involved in Multisourcing Integration project scope management, and why is good Multisourcing Integration project scope management so important on information technology Multisourcing Integration projects?

79. Is the pace of implementing the products of the program ensuring the completeness of the results of

the Multisourcing Integration project?

80. How many days can task X be late in starting without affecting the Multisourcing Integration project completion date?

81. On which process should team members spend the most time?

82. Is the Multisourcing Integration project supported by national and/or local organizations?

83. In what way has the program contributed towards the issue culture and development included on the public agenda?

84. What is a Software Development Life Cycle (SDLC)?

85. Do the partners have sufficient financial capacity to keep up the benefits produced by the programme?

86. To what extent have the target population and participants made the activities own, taking an active role in it?

87. How well did the chosen processes fit the needs of the Multisourcing Integration project?

88. Are you just doing busywork to pass the time?

89. Professionals want to know what is expected from them; what are the deliverables?

90. How does activity resource estimation affect activity duration estimation?

91. If a risk event occurs, what will you do?

2.1 Project Management Plan: Multisourcing Integration

92. What would you do differently what did not work?

93. How well are you able to manage your risk?

94. Is the budget realistic?

95. What are the assigned resources?

96. Is mitigation authorized or recommended?

97. What does management expect of PMs?

98. Are the existing and future without-plan conditions reasonable and appropriate?

99. Does the selected plan protect privacy?

100. What is Multisourcing Integration project scope management?

101. What are the known stakeholder requirements?

102. Is there an incremental analysis/cost effectiveness analysis of proposed mitigation features based on an approved method and using an accepted model?

103. Has the selected plan been formulated using cost effectiveness and incremental analysis techniques?

104. What data/reports/tools/etc. do program managers need?

105. What went wrong?

106. Why Change?

107. Are there non-structural buyout or relocation recommendations?

108. Development trends and opportunities. What if the positive direction and vision of your organization causes expected trends to change?

109. Are calculations and results of analyzes essentially correct?

2.2 Scope Management Plan: Multisourcing Integration

110. Describe the manner in which Multisourcing Integration project deliverables will be formally presented and accepted. Will they be presented at the end of each phase?

111. Has the scope management document been updated and distributed to help prevent scope creep?

112. Do all stakeholders know how to access this repository and where to find the Multisourcing Integration project documentation?

113. Are actuals compared against estimates to analyze and correct variances?

114. What is the estimated cost of creating and implementing?

115. Is your organization structure for both tracking & controlling the budget well defined and assigned to a specific individual?

116. Was the scope definition used in task sequencing?

117. Given the scope of the Multisourcing Integration project, which criterion should be optimized?

118. Have the key functions and capabilities been defined and assigned to each release or iteration?

119. Why do you need to manage scope?

120. What are the risks that could significantly affect the resources needed for the Multisourcing Integration project?

121. Has a proper Multisourcing Integration project work location been established that will allow the team to work together with user personnel?

122. Are there any windfall benefits that would accrue to the Multisourcing Integration project sponsor or other parties?

123. Cost / benefit analysis?

124. How many changes are you making?

125. What do you need to do to accomplish the goal or goals?

126. Is the assigned Multisourcing Integration project manager a PMP (Certified Multisourcing Integration project manager) and experienced?

127. Does the resource management plan include a personnel development plan?

128. Do you document disagreements and work towards resolutions?

129. What should you drop in order to add something new?

2.3 Requirements Management Plan: Multisourcing Integration

130. Will the contractors involved take full responsibility?

131. Did you get proper approvals?

132. How will bidders price evaluations be done, by deliverables, phases, or in a big bang?

133. What are you counting on?

134. How detailed should the Multisourcing Integration project get?

135. Who came up with this requirement?

136. Do you really need to write this document at all?

137. What went right?

138. Is the change control process documented?

139. What cost metrics will be used?

140. Could inaccurate or incomplete requirements in this Multisourcing Integration project create a serious risk for the business?

141. Does the Multisourcing Integration project have a Change Control process?

142. Did you provide clear and concise specifications?

143. Will the product release be stable and mature enough to be deployed in the user community?

144. Is the user satisfied?

145. What information regarding the Multisourcing Integration project requirements will be reported?

146. Is stakeholder risk tolerance an important factor for the requirements process in this Multisourcing Integration project?

147. Is it new or replacing an existing business system or process?

148. What performance metrics will be used?

149. Will you perform a Requirements Risk assessment and develop a plan to deal with risks?

2.4 Requirements Documentation: Multisourcing Integration

150. Can you check system requirements?

151. What variations exist for a process?

152. What happens when requirements are wrong?

153. Is the requirement realistically testable?

154. Is new technology needed?

155. What are the potential disadvantages/ advantages?

156. Where are business rules being captured?

157. What kind of entity is a problem ?

158. What are the attributes of a customer?

159. Is your business case still valid?

160. What is the risk associated with the technology?

161. Where do you define what is a customer, what are the attributes of customer?

162. How does the proposed Multisourcing Integration project contribute to the overall objectives of your organization?

163. How linear / iterative is your Requirements Gathering process (or will it be)?

164. The problem with gathering requirements is right there in the word gathering. What images does it conjure?

165. Where do system and software requirements come from, what are sources?

166. What are the acceptance criteria?

167. Who is involved?

168. Who provides requirements?

169. What will be the integration problems?

2.5 Requirements Traceability Matrix: Multisourcing Integration

170. How small is small enough?

171. What are the chronologies, contingencies, consequences, criteria?

172. How will it affect the stakeholders personally in career?

173. Why do you manage scope?

174. What is the WBS?

175. Describe the process for approving requirements so they can be added to the traceability matrix and Multisourcing Integration project work can be performed. Will the Multisourcing Integration project requirements become approved in writing?

176. Is there a requirements traceability process in place?

177. Do you have a clear understanding of all subcontracts in place?

178. Why use a WBS?

179. What percentage of Multisourcing Integration projects are producing traceability matrices between requirements and other work products?

180. How do you manage scope?

181. Will you use a Requirements Traceability Matrix?

2.6 Project Scope Statement: Multisourcing Integration

182. Have the reports to be produced, distributed, and filed been defined?

183. Have you been able to easily identify success criteria and create objective measurements for each of the Multisourcing Integration project scopes goal statements?

184. Will the qa related information be reported regularly as part of the status reporting mechanisms?

185. What is a process you might recommend to verify the accuracy of the research deliverable?

186. If there is an independent oversight contractor, have they signed off on the Multisourcing Integration project Plan?

187. How will you verify the accuracy of the work of the Multisourcing Integration project, and what constitutes acceptance of the deliverables?

188. Is the Multisourcing Integration project organization documented and on file?

189. Will the risk status be reported to management on a regular and frequent basis?

190. Is the plan for your organization of the Multisourcing Integration project resources

adequate?

191. Relevant - ask yourself can you get there; why are you doing this Multisourcing Integration project?

192. Is this process communicated to the customer and team members?

193. What is the most common tool for helping define the detail?

194. Are the input requirements from the team members clearly documented and communicated?

195. Are there completion/verification criteria defined for each task producing an output?

196. Was planning completed before the Multisourcing Integration project was initiated?

197. Is there a Change Management Board?

198. Have the configuration management functions been assigned?

199. Will the risk documents be filed?

2.7 Assumption and Constraint Log: Multisourcing Integration

200. Are there cosmetic errors that hinder readability and comprehension?

201. Are you meeting your customers expectations consistently?

202. Was the document/deliverable developed per the appropriate or required standards (for example, Institute of Electrical and Electronics Engineers standards)?

203. Is the current scope of the Multisourcing Integration project substantially different than that originally defined in the approved Multisourcing Integration project plan?

204. Are there standards for code development?

205. How can you prevent/fix violations?

206. Does the document/deliverable meet general requirements (for example, statement of work) for all deliverables?

207. Contradictory information between document sections?

208. Have all necessary approvals been obtained?

209. How can constraints be violated?

210. Violation trace: why ?

211. What worked well?

212. Does the document/deliverable meet all requirements (for example, statement of work) specific to this deliverable?

213. Have all stakeholders been identified?

214. Has a Multisourcing Integration project Communications Plan been developed?

215. What does an audit system look like?

216. Does the system design reflect the requirements?

217. Do you know what your customers expectations are regarding this process?

218. Has the approach and development strategy of the Multisourcing Integration project been defined, documented and accepted by the appropriate stakeholders?

219. What do you audit?

2.8 Work Breakdown Structure: Multisourcing Integration

220. How big is a work-package?

221. Why would you develop a Work Breakdown Structure?

222. How will you and your Multisourcing Integration project team define the Multisourcing Integration projects scope and work breakdown structure?

223. When do you stop?

224. How far down?

225. How many levels?

226. What has to be done?

227. When does it have to be done?

228. Do you need another level?

229. Where does it take place?

230. Is it still viable?

231. What is the probability that the Multisourcing Integration project duration will exceed xx weeks?

232. What is the probability of completing the Multisourcing Integration project in less that xx days?

233. Who has to do it?

234. Why is it useful?

235. Can you make it?

236. Is it a change in scope?

2.9 WBS Dictionary: Multisourcing Integration

237. Does the contractor have procedures which permit identification of recurring or non-recurring costs as necessary?

238. Is data disseminated to the contractors management timely, accurate, and usable?

239. Are the overhead pools formally and adequately identified?

240. Are the requirements for all items of overhead established by rational, traceable processes?

241. The Multisourcing Integration projected business base for each period?

242. Budgets assigned to major functional organizations?

243. Is the work done on a work package level as described in the WBS dictionary?

244. Can the contractor substantiate work package and planning package budgets?

245. Are procedures established to prevent changes to the contract budget base other than the already stated authorized by contractual action?

246. Are there procedures for monitoring action items

and corrective actions to the point of resolution and are corresponding procedures being followed?

247. The anticipated business volume?

248. Are indirect costs charged to the appropriate indirect pools and incurring organization?

249. Are overhead costs budgets established on a basis consistent with anticipated direct business base?

250. Identify potential or actual budget-based and time-based schedule variances?

251. The already stated responsible for overhead performance control of related costs?

252. Are the responsibilities and authorities of each of the above organizational elements or managers clearly defined?

253. Cwbs elements to be subcontracted, with identification of subcontractors?

254. What is the end result of a work package?

255. Are retroactive changes to direct costs and indirect costs prohibited except for the correction of errors and routine accounting adjustments?

2.10 Schedule Management Plan: Multisourcing Integration

256. Are right task and resource calendars used in the IMS?

257. Have the key elements of a coherent Multisourcing Integration project management strategy been established?

258. Was your organizations estimating methodology being used and followed?

259. Has the business need been clearly defined?

260. Were stakeholders aware and supportive of the principles and practices of modern software estimation?

261. Is a process defined to measure the performance of the schedule management process itself?

262. Is there a formal set of procedures supporting Issues Management?

263. Are procurement deliverables arriving on time and to specification?

264. Have all team members been part of identifying risks?

265. List all schedule constraints here. Must the Multisourcing Integration project be complete by a

specified date?

266. Were the budget estimates reasonable?

267. Does the Multisourcing Integration project have a Statement of Work?

268. Has a quality assurance plan been developed for the Multisourcing Integration project?

269. Are software metrics formally captured, analyzed and used as a basis for other Multisourcing Integration project estimates?

270. Have external dependencies been captured in the schedule?

271. Is there a formal process for updating the Multisourcing Integration project baseline?

272. Are the results of quality assurance reviews provided to affected groups & individuals?

273. Have Multisourcing Integration project success criteria been defined?

274. Is the schedule feasible and at what cost?

275. Is there an on-going process in place to monitor Multisourcing Integration project risks?

2.11 Activity List: Multisourcing Integration

276. What will be performed?

277. For other activities, how much delay can be tolerated?

278. What is your organizations history in doing similar activities?

279. Where will it be performed?

280. What is the total time required to complete the Multisourcing Integration project if no delays occur?

281. How difficult will it be to do specific activities on this Multisourcing Integration project?

282. What went well?

283. Should you include sub-activities?

284. How detailed should a Multisourcing Integration project get?

285. What is the LF and LS for each activity?

286. Who will perform the work?

287. When will the work be performed?

288. In what sequence?

289. What is the probability the Multisourcing Integration project can be completed in xx weeks?

290. Are the required resources available or need to be acquired?

291. The wbs is developed as part of a joint planning session. and how do you know that youhave done this right?

292. How will it be performed?

293. How much slack is available in the Multisourcing Integration project?

2.12 Activity Attributes: Multisourcing Integration

294. How difficult will it be to complete specific activities on this Multisourcing Integration project?

295. Would you consider either of corresponding activities an outlier?

296. Is there a trend during the year?

297. What is missing?

298. How many days do you need to complete the work scope with a limit of X number of resources?

299. How difficult will it be to do specific activities on this Multisourcing Integration project?

300. Were there other ways you could have organized the data to achieve similar results?

301. Have you identified the Activity Leveling Priority code value on each activity?

302. How much activity detail is required?

303. Resource is assigned to?

304. What activity do you think you should spend the most time on?

305. Does your organization of the data change its

meaning?

306. How many resources do you need to complete the work scope within a limit of X number of days?

307. Which method produces the more accurate cost assignment?

308. What conclusions/generalizations can you draw from this?

309. Time for overtime?

2.13 Milestone List: Multisourcing Integration

310. Gaps in capabilities?

311. Describe your organizations strengths and core competencies. What factors will make your organization succeed?

312. Loss of key staff?

313. Timescales, deadlines and pressures?

314. Information and research?

315. Describe the industry you are in and the market growth opportunities. What is the market for your technology, product or service?

316. Global influences?

317. Can you derive how soon can the whole Multisourcing Integration project finish?

318. What is the market for your technology, product or service?

319. How late can the activity finish?

320. Continuity, supply chain robustness?

321. Environmental effects?

322. Legislative effects?

323. Identify critical paths (one or more) and which activities are on the critical path?

324. Do you foresee any technical risks or developmental challenges?

325. New USPs?

326. Which path is the critical path?

327. How will the milestone be verified?

328. Who will manage the Multisourcing Integration project on a day-to-day basis?

329. What would happen if a delivery of material was one week late?

2.14 Network Diagram: Multisourcing Integration

330. What are the Key Success Factors?

331. Where do you schedule uncertainty time?

332. What is the probability of completing the Multisourcing Integration project in less that xx days?

333. What can be done concurrently?

334. Are the required resources available?

335. What controls the start and finish of a job?

336. Planning: who, how long, what to do?

337. Which type of network diagram allows you to depict four types of dependencies?

338. Exercise: what is the probability that the Multisourcing Integration project duration will exceed xx weeks?

339. What is the lowest cost to complete this Multisourcing Integration project in xx weeks?

340. Can you calculate the confidence level?

341. Review the logical flow of the network diagram. Take a look at which activities you have first and then sequence the activities. Do they make sense?

342. Where do schedules come from?

343. What are the Major Administrative Issues?

344. What must be completed before an activity can be started?

345. How confident can you be in your milestone dates and the delivery date?

346. Will crashing x weeks return more in benefits than it costs?

347. Are you on time?

348. What job or jobs could run concurrently?

2.15 Activity Resource Requirements: Multisourcing Integration

349. Do you use tools like decomposition and rolling-wave planning to produce the activity list and other outputs?

350. When does monitoring begin?

351. What are constraints that you might find during the Human Resource Planning process?

352. Why do you do that?

353. What is the Work Plan Standard?

354. Is there anything planned that does not need to be here?

355. How do you manage time?

356. How do you handle petty cash?

357. Anything else?

358. How many signatures do you require on a check and does this match what is in your policy and procedures?

359. Other support in specific areas?

360. Which logical relationship does the PDM use most often?

361. Are there unresolved issues that need to be addressed?

2.16 Resource Breakdown Structure: Multisourcing Integration

362. What is the number one predictor of a groups productivity?

363. What are the requirements for resource data?

364. The list could probably go on, but, the thing that you would most like to know is, How long & How much?

365. Is predictive resource analysis being done?

366. Who will use the system?

367. Who will be used as a Multisourcing Integration project team member?

368. Changes based on input from stakeholders?

369. How should the information be delivered?

370. What is the purpose of assigning and documenting responsibility?

371. How can this help you with team building?

372. Who delivers the information?

373. Why do you do it?

374. How difficult will it be to do specific activities on

this Multisourcing Integration project?

375. Who is allowed to perform which functions?

376. Goals for the Multisourcing Integration project. What is each stakeholders desired outcome for the Multisourcing Integration project?

2.17 Activity Duration Estimates: Multisourcing Integration

377. Are costs that may be needed to account for Multisourcing Integration project risks determined?

378. Are the causes of all variances identified?

379. Why is activity definition the first process involved in Multisourcing Integration project time management?

380. Do stakeholders follow a procedure for formally accepting the Multisourcing Integration project scope?

381. What are key inputs and outputs of the software?

382. Which frame seemed to be the most important and why?

383. Describe Multisourcing Integration project integration management in your own words. How does Multisourcing Integration project integration management relate to the Multisourcing Integration project life cycle, stakeholders, and the other Multisourcing Integration project management knowledge areas?

384. Does the software appear easy to learn?

385. Are actual Multisourcing Integration project results compared with planned or expected results to

determine the variance?

386. Which types of reports would help provide summary information to senior management?

387. What is the difference between % Complete and % work?

388. Why is outsourcing growing so rapidly?

389. How could you define throughput and how would your organization benefit from maximizing it?

390. What tasks must follow this task?

391. Will the new application negatively affect the current IT infrastructure?

392. How does the job market and current state of the economy affect human resource management?

393. Why is there a growing trend in outsourcing, especially in the government?

394. Are Multisourcing Integration project records organized, maintained, and assessable by Multisourcing Integration project team members?

395. Will the new application be developed using existing hardware, software, and networks?

2.18 Duration Estimating Worksheet: Multisourcing Integration

396. What is the total time required to complete the Multisourcing Integration project if no delays occur?

397. Is this operation cost effective?

398. What is next?

399. What work will be included in the Multisourcing Integration project?

400. Is the Multisourcing Integration project responsive to community need?

401. Value pocket identification & quantification what are value pockets?

402. How should ongoing costs be monitored to try to keep the Multisourcing Integration project within budget?

403. Will the Multisourcing Integration project collaborate with the local community and leverage resources?

404. Why estimate costs?

405. Is a construction detail attached (to aid in explanation)?

406. Can the Multisourcing Integration project be

constructed as planned?

407. What info is needed?

408. What is an Average Multisourcing Integration project?

409. When, then?

410. What is cost and Multisourcing Integration project cost management?

411. Why estimate time and cost?

412. Define the work as completely as possible. What work will be included in the Multisourcing Integration project?

2.19 Project Schedule: Multisourcing Integration

413. What does that mean?

414. Eliminate unnecessary activities. Are there activities that came from a template or previous Multisourcing Integration project that are not applicable on this phase of this Multisourcing Integration project?

415. Why do you need to manage Multisourcing Integration project Risk?

416. Activity charts and bar charts are graphical representations of a Multisourcing Integration project schedule ...how do they differ?

417. Verify that the update is accurate. Are all remaining durations correct?

418. Master Multisourcing Integration project schedule?

419. How can you address that situation?

420. What is risk management?

421. If you can not fix it, how do you do it differently?

422. What is risk?

423. What is the most mis-scheduled part of process?

424. Was the Multisourcing Integration project schedule reviewed by all stakeholders and formally accepted?

425. How do you use schedules?

426. Is Multisourcing Integration project work proceeding in accordance with the original Multisourcing Integration project schedule?

427. Should you have a test for each code module?

428. Did the final product meet or exceed user expectations?

429. If there are any qualifying green components to this Multisourcing Integration project, what portion of the total Multisourcing Integration project cost is green?

430. How can slack be negative?

2.20 Cost Management Plan: Multisourcing Integration

431. Are metrics used to evaluate and manage Vendors?

432. What is the work breakdown structure for the Multisourcing Integration project?

433. Have process improvement efforts been completed before requirements efforts begin?

434. If you sold 10x widgets on a day, what would the affect on costs be?

435. Are changes in scope (deliverable commitments) agreed to by all affected groups & individuals?

436. Is stakeholder involvement adequate?

437. Are Multisourcing Integration project team members involved in detailed estimating and scheduling?

438. Have key stakeholders been identified?

439. Has Multisourcing Integration project success criteria been defined?

440. Has the schedule been baselined?

441. Have the reasons why the changes to your organizational systems and capabilities are required?

442. Is the Multisourcing Integration project schedule available for all Multisourcing Integration project team members to review?

443. Are adequate resources provided for the quality assurance function?

444. Schedule variances – how will schedule variances be identified and corrected?

445. Have the procedures for identifying budget variances been followed?

446. Are any non-compliance issues that exist due to State practices communicated to your organization?

2.21 Activity Cost Estimates: Multisourcing Integration

447. What is the last item a Multisourcing Integration project manager must do to finalize Multisourcing Integration project close-out?

448. What is the activity inventory?

449. Maintenance Reserve?

450. How do you allocate indirect costs to activities?

451. How and when do you enter into Multisourcing Integration project Procurement Management?

452. What do you want to know about the stay to know if costs were inappropriately high or low?

453. Does the estimator have experience?

454. Were the costs or charges reasonable?

455. Can you delete activities or make them inactive?

456. How do you change activities?

457. Measurable - are the targets measurable?

458. Certification of actual expenditures?

459. Does the activity use a common approach or business function to deliver its results?

460. What is the activity recast of the budget?

461. What is your organizations history in doing similar tasks?

462. The impact and what actions were taken?

463. What is procurement?

2.22 Cost Estimating Worksheet: Multisourcing Integration

464. What will others want?

465. Who is best positioned to know and assist in identifying corresponding factors?

466. Will the Multisourcing Integration project collaborate with the local community and leverage resources?

467. What is the purpose of estimating?

468. How will the results be shared and to whom?

469. What is the estimated labor cost today based upon this information?

470. What happens to any remaining funds not used?

471. Identify the timeframe necessary to monitor progress and collect data to determine how the selected measure has changed?

472. What additional Multisourcing Integration project(s) could be initiated as a result of this Multisourcing Integration project?

473. Can a trend be established from historical performance data on the selected measure and are the criteria for using trend analysis or forecasting methods met?

474. Does the Multisourcing Integration project provide innovative ways for stakeholders to overcome obstacles or deliver better outcomes?

475. Ask: are others positioned to know, are others credible, and will others cooperate?

476. What can be included?

477. What costs are to be estimated?

478. Is it feasible to establish a control group arrangement?

479. Is the Multisourcing Integration project responsive to community need?

2.23 Cost Baseline: Multisourcing Integration

480. Are you meeting with your team regularly?

481. For what purpose ?

482. Have you identified skills that are missing from your team?

483. Pcs for your new business. what would the life cycle costs be?

484. Is the requested change request a result of changes in other Multisourcing Integration project(s)?

485. How likely is it to go wrong?

486. Impact to environment?

487. What threats might prevent you from getting there?

488. How accurate do cost estimates need to be?

489. Has the Multisourcing Integration project documentation been archived or otherwise disposed as described in the Multisourcing Integration project communication plan?

490. Is there anything you need from upper management in order to be successful?

491. Have all approved changes to the schedule baseline been identified and impact on the Multisourcing Integration project documented?

492. What weaknesses do you have?

493. Who will use corresponding metrics ?

494. Are procedures defined by which the cost baseline may be changed?

495. Has the documentation relating to operation and maintenance of the product(s) or service(s) been delivered to, and accepted by, operations management?

496. Has the appropriate access to relevant data and analysis capability been granted?

2.24 Quality Management Plan: Multisourcing Integration

497. What is the audience for the data?

498. After observing execution of process, is it in compliance with the documented Plan?

499. What are your key performance measures/ indicators for tracking progress relative to your action plans?

500. What is the Quality Management Plan?

501. Account for the procedures used to verify the data quality of the data being reviewed?

502. How does your organization maintain a safe and healthy work environment?

503. What key performance indicators does your organization use to measure, manage, and improve key processes?

504. Can you perform this task or activity in a more effective manner?

505. Is the process working, and people are not executing in compliance of the process?

506. Meet how often?

507. Who else should be involved ?

508. Written by multiple authors and in multiple writing styles?

509. What are you trying to accomplish?

510. Was trending evident between audits?

511. Checking the completeness and appropriateness of the sampling and testing. Were the right locations/samples tested for the right parameters?

512. How is staff informed of proper reporting methods?

513. Documented results available?

514. Does the program use modeling in the permitting or decision-making processes?

515. How does your organization recruit, hire, and retain new employees?

2.25 Quality Metrics: Multisourcing Integration

516. Are quality metrics defined?

517. Does risk analysis documentation meet standards?

518. What level of statistical confidence do you use?

519. The metrics–what is being considered?

520. Are there any open risk issues?

521. Is quality culture a competitive advantage?

522. Which are the right metrics to use?

523. What documentation is required?

524. Where did complaints, returns and warranty claims come from?

525. Is a risk containment plan in place?

526. Have alternatives been defined in the event that failure occurs?

527. Is there a set of procedures to capture, analyze and act on quality metrics?

528. Are interface issues coordinated?

529. How do you calculate corresponding metrics?

530. What metrics are important and most beneficial to measure?

531. What happens if you get an abnormal result?

532. Do you know how much profit a 10% decrease in waste would generate?

533. Subjective quality component: customer satisfaction, how do you measure it?

534. What approved evidence based screening tools can be used?

535. What metrics do you measure?

2.26 Process Improvement Plan: Multisourcing Integration

536. Are you making progress on the improvement framework?

537. Have the frequency of collection and the points in the process where measurements will be made been determined?

538. Are you meeting the quality standards?

539. Where are you now?

540. Are you making progress on the goals?

541. Have the supporting tools been developed or acquired?

542. Everyone agrees on what process improvement is, right?

543. Where do you focus?

544. Modeling current processes is great, and will you ever see a return on that investment?

545. What actions are needed to address the problems and achieve the goals?

546. Management commitment at all levels?

547. Why do you want to achieve the goal?

548. Have storage and access mechanisms and procedures been determined?

549. How do you measure?

550. What is the return on investment?

551. The motive is determined by asking, Why do you want to achieve this goal?

552. What lessons have you learned so far?

553. Purpose of goal: the motive is determined by asking, why do you want to achieve this goal?

554. What personnel are the sponsors for that initiative?

2.27 Responsibility Assignment Matrix: Multisourcing Integration

555. Will too many Communicating responsibilities tangle the Multisourcing Integration project in unnecessary communications?

556. How cost benefit analysis?

557. Are data elements reconcilable between internal summary reports and reports forwarded to stakeholders?

558. Does the contractors system provide unit or lot costs when applicable?

559. Do you know how your people are allocated?

560. Who is the sponsor?

561. What expertise is available in your department?

562. Does the contractors system include procedures for measuring the performance of critical subcontractors?

563. Most people let you know when others re too busy, and are others really too busy?

564. Performance to date and material commitment?

565. Too many is: do all the identified roles need to be routinely informed or only in exceptional

circumstances?

566. Are overhead cost budgets established for each organization which has authority to incur overhead costs?

567. Changes in the current direct and Multisourcing Integration projected base?

568. Ideas for developing soft skills at your organization?

569. Are material costs reported within the same period as that in which BCWP is earned for that material?

570. The staff interests – is the group or the person interested in working for this Multisourcing Integration project?

2.28 Roles and Responsibilities: Multisourcing Integration

571. Accountabilities: what are the roles and responsibilities of individual team members?

572. Required skills, knowledge, experience?

573. Was the expectation clearly communicated?

574. What should you highlight for improvement?

575. What should you do now to prepare yourself for a promotion, increased responsibilities or a different job?

576. How is your work-life balance?

577. Once the responsibilities are defined for the Multisourcing Integration project, have the deliverables, roles and responsibilities been clearly communicated to every participant?

578. Does the team have access to and ability to use data analysis tools?

579. Concern: where are you limited or have no authority, where you can not influence?

580. Do you take the time to clearly define roles and responsibilities on Multisourcing Integration project tasks?

581. What specific behaviors did you observe?

582. Implementation of actions: Who are the responsible units?

583. Are the quality assurance functions and related roles and responsibilities clearly defined?

584. Do the values and practices inherent in the culture of your organization foster or hinder the process?

585. What should you do now to ensure that you are meeting all expectations of your current position?

586. How well did the Multisourcing Integration project Team understand the expectations of specific roles and responsibilities?

587. Attainable / achievable: the goal is attainable; can you actually accomplish the goal?

588. What is working well?

2.29 Human Resource Management Plan: Multisourcing Integration

589. Has a resource management plan been created?

590. Pareto diagrams, statistical sampling, flow charting or trend analysis used quality monitoring?

591. Does the Multisourcing Integration project have a formal Multisourcing Integration project Charter?

592. What were things that you need to improve?

593. Does the business case include how the Multisourcing Integration project aligns with your organizations strategic goals & objectives?

594. Do Multisourcing Integration project managers participating in the Multisourcing Integration project know the Multisourcing Integration projects true status first hand?

595. What were things that you did very well and want to do the same again on the next Multisourcing Integration project?

596. Personnel with expertise?

597. Were Multisourcing Integration project team members involved in detailed estimating and scheduling?

598. Is there any form of automated support for Issues

Management?

599. Do people have the competencies to meet the strategic objectives?

600. Are key risk mitigation strategies added to the Multisourcing Integration project schedule?

601. Are vendor contract reports, reviews and visits conducted periodically?

602. Timeline and milestones?

603. Who needs training?

604. Is quality monitored from the perspective of the customers needs and expectations?

605. Is there general agreement & acceptance of the current status and progress of the Multisourcing Integration project?

606. Are changes in deliverable commitments agreed to by all affected groups & individuals?

607. Responsiveness to change and the resulting demands for different skills and abilities?

608. Are meeting objectives identified for each meeting?

2.30 Communications Management Plan: Multisourcing Integration

609. What steps can you take for a positive relationship?

610. Do you ask; can you recommend others for you to talk with about this initiative?

611. Are others needed?

612. Are others part of the communications management plan?

613. What is the stakeholders level of authority?

614. Which stakeholders can influence others?

615. Do you prepare stakeholder engagement plans?

616. How much time does it take to do it?

617. What are the interrelationships?

618. Do you feel more overwhelmed by stakeholders?

619. Why do you manage communications?

620. Why manage stakeholders?

621. Who were proponents/opponents?

622. Who have you worked with in past, similar

initiatives?

623. How did the term stakeholder originate?

624. How is this initiative related to other portfolios, programs, or Multisourcing Integration projects?

625. Who needs to know and how much?

626. What is Multisourcing Integration project communications management?

627. What is the political influence?

628. Is there an important stakeholder who is actively opposed and will not receive messages?

2.31 Risk Management Plan: Multisourcing Integration

629. Are people attending meetings and doing work?

630. Are tools for analysis and design available?

631. How can you fix it?

632. Financial risk: can your organization afford to undertake the Multisourcing Integration project?

633. Are team members trained in the use of the tools?

634. What can you do to minimize the impact if it does?

635. What are the cost, schedule and resource impacts of avoiding the risk?

636. Do requirements demand the use of new analysis, design, or testing methods?

637. Is the customer willing to participate in reviews?

638. Mitigation -how can you avoid the risk?

639. What risks are tracked?

640. Is the customer willing to commit significant time to the requirements gathering process?

641. How can the process be made more effective or less cumbersome (process improvements)?

642. Are there risks to human health or the environment that need to be controlled or mitigated?

643. Monitoring -what factors can you track that will enable you to determine if the risk is becoming more or less likely?

644. Is the customer technically sophisticated in the product area?

645. Why might it be late?

646. Are the reports useful and easy to read?

647. How is implementation of risk actions performed?

648. How quickly does this item need to be resolved?

2.32 Risk Register: Multisourcing Integration

649. Risk probability and impact: how will the probabilities and impacts of risk items be assessed?

650. When is it going to be done?

651. Having taken action, how did the responses effect change, and where is the Multisourcing Integration project now?

652. What are your key risks/show istoppers and what is being done to manage them?

653. Financial risk -can your organization afford to undertake the Multisourcing Integration project?

654. User involvement: do you have the right users?

655. What may happen or not go according to plan?

656. What are the assumptions and current status that support the assessment of the risk?

657. Have other controls and solutions been implemented in other services which could be applied as an alternative to additional funding?

658. What has changed since the last period?

659. What is your current and future risk profile?

660. Who needs to know about this?

661. Assume the risk event or situation happens, what would the impact be?

662. What evidence do you have to justify the likelihood score of the risk (audit, incident report, claim, complaints, inspection, internal review)?

663. What are you going to do to limit the Multisourcing Integration projects risk exposure due to the identified risks?

664. Contingency actions - planned actions to reduce the immediate seriousness of the risk when it does occur. What should you do when?

665. What should you do when?

666. Recovery actions - planned actions taken once a risk has occurred to allow you to move on. What should you do after?

667. Which key risks have ineffective responses or outstanding improvement actions?

668. What should the audit role be in establishing a risk management process?

2.33 Probability and Impact Assessment: Multisourcing Integration

669. What are the current requirements of the customer?

670. Assuming that you have identified a number of risks in the Multisourcing Integration project, how would you prioritize them?

671. What is the level of experience available with your organization?

672. Are there new risks that mitigation strategies might introduce?

673. Have staff received necessary training?

674. What should be the level of difficulty in handling the technology?

675. What are the chances the event will occur?

676. What are your data sources?

677. What will be the environmental impact of the Multisourcing Integration project?

678. How is risk handled within this Multisourcing Integration project organization?

679. Can the Multisourcing Integration project

proceed without assuming the risk?

680. How do you maximize short-term return on investment?

681. Are trained personnel, including supervisors and Multisourcing Integration project managers, available to handle such a large Multisourcing Integration project?

682. Do you have a consistent repeatable process that is actually used?

683. Do the requirements require the creation of new algorithms?

684. What will be the impact or consequence if the risk occurs?

685. What action do you usually take against risks?

686. Are the risk data complete?

687. What kind of preparation would be required to do this?

2.34 Probability and Impact Matrix: Multisourcing Integration

688. What is the probability of the risk occurring?

689. What are the current or emerging trends of culture?

690. Could others have been better mitigated?

691. Mandated delivery date?

692. What will be the environmental impact of the Multisourcing Integration project?

693. How would you define a risk?

694. Is a software Multisourcing Integration project management tool available?

695. How are you working with risks?

696. Can you handle the investment risk?

697. How should you structure risks?

698. Which role do you have in the Multisourcing Integration project?

699. What should be done with risks on the watch list?

700. What can go wrong?

701. Prioritized components/features?

702. During which risk management process is a determination to transfer a risk made?

703. Can it be enlarged by drawing people from other areas of your organization?

704. Have you ascribed a level of confidence to every critical technical objective?

705. What will be cost of redeployment of the personnel?

706. What is Multisourcing Integration project risk management?

2.35 Risk Data Sheet: Multisourcing Integration

707. What are you here for (Mission)?

708. What can you do?

709. How can it happen?

710. Is the data sufficiently specified in terms of the type of failure being analyzed, and its frequency or probability?

711. How do you handle product safely?

712. Do effective diagnostic tests exist?

713. Potential for recurrence?

714. Who has a vested interest in how you perform as your organization (our stakeholders)?

715. What are you weak at and therefore need to do better?

716. Are new hazards created?

717. What is the likelihood of it happening?

718. What was measured?

719. Whom do you serve (customers)?

720. What are the main threats to your existence?

721. What will be the consequences if it happens?

722. What if client refuses?

723. Risk of what?

724. What are you trying to achieve (Objectives)?

725. If it happens, what are the consequences?

726. How reliable is the data source?

2.36 Procurement Management Plan: Multisourcing Integration

727. How will the duration of the Multisourcing Integration project influence your decisions?

728. Why is procurement planning important?

729. Have lessons learned been conducted after each Multisourcing Integration project release?

730. Were Multisourcing Integration project team members involved in detailed estimating and scheduling?

731. Are trade-offs between accepting the risk and mitigating the risk identified?

732. Have reserves been created to address risks?

733. Have stakeholder accountabilities & responsibilities been clearly defined?

734. Does the detailed work plan match the complexity of tasks with the capabilities of personnel?

735. Are all payments made according to the contract(s)?

736. Is there a procurement management plan in place?

737. Is there an onboarding process in place?

738. Are target dates established for each milestone deliverable?

739. Similar Multisourcing Integration projects?

740. Are decisions captured in a decisions log?

741. Are the Multisourcing Integration project plans updated on a frequent basis?

742. Is Multisourcing Integration project status reviewed with the steering and executive teams at appropriate intervals?

2.37 Source Selection Criteria: Multisourcing Integration

743. Is a letter of commitment from each proposed team member and key subcontractor included?

744. Does your documentation identify why the team concurs or differs with reported performance from past performance report (CPARs, questionnaire responses, etc.)?

745. Is this a cost contract?

746. What are the steps in performing a cost/tech tradeoff?

747. What should clarifications include?

748. What documentation is necessary regarding electronic communications?

749. Are there any common areas of weaknesses or deficiencies in the proposals in the competitive range?

750. What source selection software is your team using?

751. How should oral presentations be evaluated?

752. How long will it take for the purchase cost to be the same as the lease cost?

753. In the technical/management area, what criteria do you use to determine the final evaluation ratings?

754. What are the guidelines regarding award without considerations?

755. What is price analysis and when should it be performed?

756. Have team members been adequately trained?

757. Who is entitled to a debriefing?

758. How will you evaluate offerors proposals?

759. What will you use to capture evaluation and subsequent documentation?

760. Why promote competition?

761. Are responses to considerations adequate?

762. What does a sample rating scale look like?

2.38 Stakeholder Management Plan: Multisourcing Integration

763. Are estimating assumptions and constraints captured?

764. Are the payment terms being followed?

765. Does all Multisourcing Integration project documentation reside in a common repository for easy access?

766. Are internal Multisourcing Integration project status meetings held at reasonable intervals?

767. If a problem has been detected, what tools can be used to determine a root cause?

768. Where to get additional help?

769. Are tasks tracked by hours?

770. Are communication systems currently in place appropriate?

771. When would you develop a Multisourcing Integration project Business Plan?

772. Does the Multisourcing Integration project have a Quality Culture?

773. Are vendor invoices audited for accuracy before payment?

774. Will all outputs delivered by the Multisourcing Integration project follow the same process?

775. Are updated Multisourcing Integration project time & resource estimates reasonable based on the current Multisourcing Integration project stage?

776. Who is accountable for the achievement of the targeted outcome(s) and reports on the progress towards the target?

777. Does the Multisourcing Integration project have a Quality Culture?

778. Is the amount of effort justified by the anticipated value of forming a new process?

779. Were Multisourcing Integration project team members involved in the development of activity & task decomposition?

780. Is there general agreement & acceptance of the current status and progress of the Multisourcing Integration project?

2.39 Change Management Plan: Multisourcing Integration

781. What are the major changes to processes?

782. What will be the preferred method of delivery?

783. Who might be able to help you the most?

784. How will the stakeholders share information and transfer knowledge?

785. When should a given message be communicated?

786. Do you need new systems?

787. What is the worst thing that can happen if you chose not to communicate this information?

788. What would be an estimate of the total cost for the activities required to carry out the change initiative?

789. Where do you want to be?

790. What is the most positive interpretation it can receive?

791. Who in the business it includes?

792. Has a training need analysis been carried out?

793. What risks may occur upfront, during implementation and after implementation?

794. Will all field readiness criteria have been practically met prior to training roll-out?

795. What prerequisite knowledge or training is required?

796. What risks may occur upfront?

797. Readiness -what is a successful end state?

798. How do you gain sponsors buy-in to the communication plan?

799. Identify the risk and assess the significance and likelihood of it occurring and plan the contingency What risks may occur upfront?

800. What are the needs, priorities and special interests of the audience?

3.0 Executing Process Group: Multisourcing Integration

801. Why should Multisourcing Integration project managers strive to make jobs look easy?

802. What is the critical path for this Multisourcing Integration project and how long is it?

803. How many different communication channels does the Multisourcing Integration project team have?

804. What factors are contributing to progress or delay in the achievement of products and results?

805. What are the main types of goods and services being outsourced?

806. When is the appropriate time to bring the scorecard to Board meetings?

807. What is in place for ensuring adequate change control on Multisourcing Integration projects that involve outside contracts?

808. How do you prevent staff are just doing busywork to pass the time?

809. Based on your Multisourcing Integration project communication management plan, what worked well?

810. What are the main types of contracts if you do decide to outsource?

811. Does the Multisourcing Integration project team have enough people to execute the Multisourcing Integration project plan?

812. Why is it important to determine activity sequencing on Multisourcing Integration projects?

813. Do Multisourcing Integration project managers understand your organizational context for Multisourcing Integration projects?

814. Is the Multisourcing Integration project performing better or worse than planned?

815. What are some crucial elements of a good Multisourcing Integration project plan?

816. Are escalated issues resolved promptly?

817. What are crucial elements of successful Multisourcing Integration project plan execution?

818. Specific - is the objective clear in terms of what, how, when, and where the situation will be changed?

819. How could stakeholders negatively impact your Multisourcing Integration project?

3.1 Team Member Status Report: Multisourcing Integration

820. How can you make it practical?

821. How does this product, good, or service meet the needs of the Multisourcing Integration project and your organization as a whole?

822. Do you have an Enterprise Multisourcing Integration project Management Office (EPMO)?

823. What specific interest groups do you have in place?

824. Does every department have to have a Multisourcing Integration project Manager on staff?

825. Are the attitudes of staff regarding Multisourcing Integration project work improving?

826. Are the products of your organizations Multisourcing Integration projects meeting customers objectives?

827. Are your organizations Multisourcing Integration projects more successful over time?

828. Is there evidence that staff is taking a more professional approach toward management of your organizations Multisourcing Integration projects?

829. How it is to be done?

830. What is to be done?

831. Why is it to be done?

832. Will the staff do training or is that done by a third party?

833. When a teams productivity and success depend on collaboration and the efficient flow of information, what generally fails them?

834. Does the product, good, or service already exist within your organization?

835. Does your organization have the means (staff, money, contract, etc.) to produce or to acquire the product, good, or service?

836. How much risk is involved?

837. How will resource planning be done?

838. The problem with Reward & Recognition Programs is that the truly deserving people all too often get left out. How can you make it practical?

3.2 Change Request: Multisourcing Integration

839. Describe how modifications, enhancements, defects and/or deficiencies shall be notified (e.g. Problem Reports, Change Requests etc) and managed. Detail warranty and/or maintenance periods?

840. Should staff call into the helpdesk or go to the website?

841. How many lines of code must be changed to implement the change?

842. What is the relationship between requirements attributes and reliability?

843. When to submit a change request?

844. Are there requirements attributes that are strongly related to the occurrence of defects and failures?

845. Has a formal technical review been conducted to assess technical correctness?

846. Does the schedule include Multisourcing Integration project management time and change request analysis time?

847. Since there are no change requests in your Multisourcing Integration project at this point, what

must you have before you begin?

848. Are you implementing itil processes?

849. Who can suggest changes?

850. How is the change documented (format, content, storage)?

851. Who is included in the change control team?

852. Should a more thorough impact analysis be conducted?

853. Why control change across the life cycle?

854. Who needs to approve change requests?

855. How to get changes (code) out in a timely manner?

856. Why were your requested changes rejected or not made?

857. What has an inspector to inspect and to check?

3.3 Change Log: Multisourcing Integration

858. When was the request approved?

859. How does this change affect the timeline of the schedule?

860. Do the described changes impact on the integrity or security of the system?

861. Does the suggested change request seem to represent a necessary enhancement to the product?

862. Is this a mandatory replacement?

863. Is the requested change request a result of changes in other Multisourcing Integration project(s)?

864. Does the suggested change request represent a desired enhancement to the products functionality?

865. Is the submitted change a new change or a modification of a previously approved change?

866. Will the Multisourcing Integration project fail if the change request is not executed?

867. Is the change backward compatible without limitations?

868. Where do changes come from?

869. How does this change affect scope?

870. How does this relate to the standards developed for specific business processes?

871. When was the request submitted?

872. Who initiated the change request?

873. Is the change request within Multisourcing Integration project scope?

874. Is the change request open, closed or pending?

3.4 Decision Log: Multisourcing Integration

875. With whom was the decision shared or considered?

876. How does provision of information, both in terms of content and presentation, influence acceptance of alternative strategies?

877. At what point in time does loss become unacceptable?

878. What eDiscovery problem or issue did your organization set out to fix or make better?

879. How do you define success?

880. Does anything need to be adjusted?

881. Who will be given a copy of this document and where will it be kept?

882. Is your opponent open to a non-traditional workflow, or will it likely challenge anything you do?

883. How does an increasing emphasis on cost containment influence the strategies and tactics used?

884. What is the average size of your matters in an applicable measurement?

885. Behaviors; what are guidelines that the team has identified that will assist them with getting the most out of team meetings?

886. Is everything working as expected?

887. How consolidated and comprehensive a story can you tell by capturing currently available incident data in a central location and through a log of key decisions during an incident?

888. What was the rationale for the decision?

889. What are the cost implications?

890. It becomes critical to track and periodically revisit both operational effectiveness; Are you noticing all that you need to, and are you interpreting what you see effectively?

891. Which variables make a critical difference?

892. How do you know when you are achieving it?

893. What is the line where eDiscovery ends and document review begins?

894. Adversarial environment. is your opponent open to a non-traditional workflow, or will it likely challenge anything you do?

3.5 Quality Audit: Multisourcing Integration

895. What is your organizations greatest strength?

896. Is quality audit a prerequisite for program accreditation or program recognition?

897. How does your organization know that its relationship with its (past) staff is appropriately effective and constructive?

898. How does your organization know that its system for recruiting the best staff possible are appropriately effective and constructive?

899. How does your organization know that its system for ensuring that its training activities are appropriately resourced and support is appropriately effective and constructive?

900. How does your organization know that its promotions system is appropriately effective, constructive and fair?

901. Are all employees made aware of device defects which may occur from the improper performance of specific jobs?

902. Is the continuing professional education of key personnel account fored in detail?

903. How does your organization know that its

security arrangements are appropriately effective and constructive?

904. How is the Strategic Plan (and other plans) reviewed and revised?

905. How does the organization know that its system for maintaining and advancing the capabilities of its staff, particularly in relation to the Mission of the organization, is appropriately effective and constructive?

906. How does your organization know that its system for ensuring a positive organizational climate is appropriately effective and constructive?

907. How does your organization know that its staff financial services are appropriately effective and constructive?

908. What does an analysis of your organizations staff profile suggest in terms of its planning, and how is this being addressed?

909. How does your organization know that it provides a safe and healthy environment?

910. Is progress against the intentions measurable?

911. For each device to be reconditioned, are device specifications, such as appropriate engineering drawings, component specifications and software specifications, maintained?

912. How does your organization know that its research funding systems are appropriately effective

and constructive in enabling quality research outcomes?

913. Have personnel cleanliness and health requirements been established?

914. How does your organization know that its general support services planning and management systems are appropriately effective and constructive?

3.6 Team Directory: Multisourcing Integration

915. Does a Multisourcing Integration project team directory list all resources assigned to the Multisourcing Integration project?

916. Where should the information be distributed?

917. Timing: when do the effects of communication take place?

918. How will you accomplish and manage the objectives?

919. Process decisions: are contractors adequately prosecuting the work?

920. Where will the product be used and/or delivered or built when appropriate?

921. Process decisions: which organizational elements and which individuals will be assigned management functions?

922. When will you produce deliverables?

923. Who are the Team Members?

924. Who will report Multisourcing Integration project status to all stakeholders?

925. Who will be the stakeholders on your next

Multisourcing Integration project?

926. Have you decided when to celebrate the Multisourcing Integration projects completion date?

927. Who will write the meeting minutes and distribute?

928. Who will talk to the customer?

929. Process decisions: is work progressing on schedule and per contract requirements?

930. How does the team resolve conflicts and ensure tasks are completed?

931. Is construction on schedule?

932. When does information need to be distributed?

3.7 Team Operating Agreement: Multisourcing Integration

933. To whom do you deliver your services?

934. How will you divide work equitably?

935. Reimbursements: how will the team members be reimbursed for expenses and time commitments?

936. Methodologies: how will key team processes be implemented, such as training, research, work deliverable production, review and approval processes, knowledge management, and meeting procedures?

937. Are there the right people on your team?

938. Does your team need access to all documents and information at all times?

939. Resource allocation: how will individual team members account for time and expenses, and how will this be allocated in the team budget?

940. Did you determine the technology methods that best match the messages to be communicated?

941. Do you vary your voice pace, tone and pitch to engage participants and gain involvement?

942. Do you solicit member feedback about meetings and what would make them better?

943. What types of accommodations will be formulated and put in place for sustaining the team?

944. Did you recap the meeting purpose, time, and expectations?

945. Seconds for members to respond?

946. Do you brief absent members after they view meeting notes or listen to a recording?

947. How will your group handle planned absences?

948. Do you upload presentation materials in advance and test the technology?

949. Are there differences in access to communication and collaboration technology based on team member location?

950. Do you send out the agenda and meeting materials in advance?

951. What is a Virtual Team?

3.8 Team Performance Assessment: Multisourcing Integration

952. To what degree does the teams approach to its work allow for modification and improvement over time?

953. To what degree are fresh input and perspectives systematically caught and added (for example, through information and analysis, new members, and senior sponsors)?

954. If you are worried about method variance before you collect data, what sort of design elements might you include to reduce or eliminate the threat of method variance?

955. To what degree do the goals specify concrete team work products?

956. To what degree does the teams work approach provide opportunity for members to engage in open interaction?

957. To what degree can team members meet frequently enough to accomplish the teams ends?

958. To what degree are the members clear on what they are individually responsible for and what they are jointly responsible for?

959. How do you manage human resources?

960. How do you keep key people outside the group informed about its accomplishments?

961. Social categorization and intergroup behaviour: Does minimal intergroup discrimination make social identity more positive?

962. How much interpersonal friction is there in your team?

963. To what degree can team members vigorously define the teams purpose in considerations with others who are not part of the functioning team?

964. To what degree do team members understand one anothers roles and skills?

965. To what degree will new and supplemental skills be introduced as the need is recognized?

966. How hard did you try to make a good selection?

967. If you have criticized someones work for method variance in your role as reviewer, what was the circumstance?

968. Which situations call for a more extreme type of adaptiveness in which team members actually re-define roles?

969. Can familiarity breed backup?

970. To what degree are staff involved as partners in the improvement process?

971. What do you think is the most constructive thing

that could be done now to resolve considerations and disputes about method variance?

3.9 Team Member Performance Assessment: Multisourcing Integration

972. What stakeholders must be involved in the development and oversight of the performance plan?

973. Does adaptive training work?

974. Does platform-specific assessment information contribute to training placement or tailoring of instruction (e.g. aptitude-treatment interaction)?

975. What happens if a team member disagrees with the Job Expectations?

976. Can your organization rate by exception and assume that most employees are performing at an acceptable level?

977. What tools are available to determine whether all contract functional and compliance areas of performance objectives, measures, and incentives have been met?

978. How are assessments designed, delivered, and otherwise used to maximize training?

979. How should adaptive assessments be implemented?

980. To what degree do team members frequently explore the teams purpose and its implications?

981. To what degree are the skill areas critical to team performance present?

982. How often are assessments to be conducted?

983. How is performance assessment used in making future award decisions including options and extend/compete decisions?

984. To what degree can all members engage in open and interactive considerations?

985. Are the draft goals SMART ?

986. What is used as a basis for instructional decisions?

987. To what degree does the teams purpose contain themes that are particularly meaningful and memorable?

988. What evidence supports your decision-making?

989. To what degree are the relative importance and priority of the goals clear to all team members?

990. To what extent are systems and applications (e.g., game engine, mobile device platform) utilized?

991. What are the standards or expectations for success?

3.10 Issue Log: Multisourcing Integration

992. Who is the stakeholder?

993. Do you have members of your team responsible for certain stakeholders?

994. Are the Multisourcing Integration project issues uniquely identified, including to which product they refer?

995. What steps can you take for positive relationships?

996. What is a Stakeholder?

997. What is the impact on the risks?

998. Who is the issue assigned to?

999. What effort will a change need?

1000. In classifying stakeholders, which approach to do so are you using?

1001. Who is involved as you identify stakeholders?

1002. Why do you manage human resources?

1003. Is the issue log kept in a safe place?

1004. Are there too many who have an interest in

some aspect of your work?

1005. Are they needed?

1006. Are you constantly rushing from meeting to meeting?

1007. Are stakeholder roles recognized by your organization?

4.0 Monitoring and Controlling Process Group: Multisourcing Integration

1008. Do the products created live up to the necessary quality?

1009. When will the Multisourcing Integration project be done?

1010. How was the program set-up initiated?

1011. Are there areas that need improvement?

1012. Is there adequate validation on required fields?

1013. What input will you be required to provide the Multisourcing Integration project team?

1014. What areas does the group agree are the biggest success on the Multisourcing Integration project?

1015. Who are the Multisourcing Integration project stakeholders?

1016. What resources (both financial and non-financial) are available/needed?

1017. What good practices or successful experiences or transferable examples have been identified?

1018. What do they need to know about the

Multisourcing Integration project?

1019. Who needs to be engaged upfront to ensure use of results?

1020. Is progress on outcomes due to your program?

1021. Is the verbiage used appropriate and understandable?

1022. Overall, how does the program function to serve the clients?

1023. What kinds of things in particular are you looking for data on?

1024. User: who wants the information and what are they interested in?

4.1 Project Performance Report: Multisourcing Integration

1025. To what degree can team members frequently and easily communicate with one another?

1026. What is the PRS?

1027. To what degree does the formal organization make use of individual resources and meet individual needs?

1028. To what degree is there a sense that only the team can succeed?

1029. To what degree does the information network provide individuals with the information they require?

1030. To what degree can the cognitive capacity of individuals accommodate the flow of information?

1031. To what degree do all members feel responsible for all agreed-upon measures?

1032. To what degree do the structures of the formal organization motivate taskrelevant behavior and facilitate task completion?

1033. To what degree are the structures of the formal organization consistent with the behaviors in the informal organization?

1034. To what degree is there centralized control of

information sharing?

1035. To what degree do members articulate the goals beyond the team membership?

1036. To what degree does the teams work approach provide opportunity for members to engage in fact-based problem solving?

1037. To what degree do individual skills and abilities match task demands?

1038. To what degree is the information network consistent with the structure of the formal organization?

1039. To what degree does the teams purpose constitute a broader, deeper aspiration than just accomplishing short-term goals?

1040. To what degree do team members articulate the teams work approach?

4.2 Variance Analysis: Multisourcing Integration

1041. Did an existing competitor change strategy?

1042. What is the dollar amount of the fluctuation?

1043. Do the rates and prices remain constant throughout the year?

1044. What is the total budget for the Multisourcing Integration project (including estimates for authorized and unpriced work)?

1045. Do you identify potential or actual budget-based and time-based schedule variances?

1046. What business event causes fluctuations?

1047. Does the accounting system provide a basis for auditing records of direct costs chargeable to the contract?

1048. Can process improvements lead to unfavorable variances?

1049. Who are responsible for the establishment of budgets and assignment of resources for overhead performance?

1050. When, during the last four quarters, did a primary business event occur causing a fluctuation?

1051. How does the monthly budget compare to the actual experience?

1052. What is the actual cost of work performed?

1053. Are procedures for variance analysis documented and consistently applied at the control account level and selected WBS and organizational levels at least monthly as a routine task?

1054. Are records maintained to show how undistributed budgets are controlled?

1055. Are estimates of costs at completion generated in a rational, consistent manner?

1056. Why are standard cost systems used?

1057. At what point should variances be isolated and brought to the attention of the management?

4.3 Earned Value Status: Multisourcing Integration

1058. Validation is a process of ensuring that the developed system will actually achieve the stakeholders desired outcomes; Are you building the right product? What do you validate?

1059. How does this compare with other Multisourcing Integration projects?

1060. Are you hitting your Multisourcing Integration projects targets?

1061. When is it going to finish?

1062. What is the unit of forecast value?

1063. If earned value management (EVM) is so good in determining the true status of a Multisourcing Integration project and Multisourcing Integration project its completion, why is it that hardly any one uses it in information systems related Multisourcing Integration projects?

1064. Verification is a process of ensuring that the developed system satisfies the stakeholders agreements and specifications; Are you building the product right? What do you verify?

1065. How much is it going to cost by the finish?

1066. Earned value can be used in almost any

Multisourcing Integration project situation and in almost any Multisourcing Integration project environment. it may be used on large Multisourcing Integration projects, medium sized Multisourcing Integration projects, tiny Multisourcing Integration projects (in cut-down form), complex and simple Multisourcing Integration projects and in any market sector. some people, of course, know all about earned value, they have used it for years - but perhaps not as effectively as they could have?

1067. Where is evidence-based earned value in your organization reported?

1068. Where are your problem areas?

4.4 Risk Audit: Multisourcing Integration

1069. Are tool mentors available?

1070. Is the technology to be built new to your organization?

1071. To what extent are auditors effective at linking business risks and management assertions?

1072. Is there (or should there be) some impact on the process of setting materiality when the auditor more effectively identifies higher risk areas of the financial statements?

1073. What responsibilities for quality, errors, and outcomes have been delegated to staff (or others) without adequate oversight?

1074. Have risks been considered with an insurance broker or provider and suitable insurance cover been arranged?

1075. Who is responsible for what?

1076. Risks with Multisourcing Integration projects or new initiatives?

1077. Are all participants informed of safety issues?

1078. Are regular safety inspections made of buildings, grounds and equipment?

1079. What are risks and how do you manage them?

1080. Do you have proper induction processes for all new paid staff and volunteers who have a specific role and responsibility?

1081. Estimated size of product in number of programs, files, transactions?

1082. Are testing tools available and suitable?

1083. Are formal technical reviews part of this process?

1084. Does the implementation method matter?

1085. Have you reviewed your constitution within the last twelve months?

1086. Are end-users enthusiastically committed to the Multisourcing Integration project and the system/product to be built?

1087. Management -what contingency plans do you have if the risk becomes a reality?

1088. How effective are your risk controls?

4.5 Contractor Status Report: Multisourcing Integration

1089. What was the budget or estimated cost for your organizations services?

1090. How does the proposed individual meet each requirement?

1091. What is the average response time for answering a support call?

1092. How is risk transferred?

1093. What was the actual budget or estimated cost for your organizations services?

1094. What was the overall budget or estimated cost?

1095. Are there contractual transfer concerns?

1096. If applicable; describe your standard schedule for new software version releases. Are new software version releases included in the standard maintenance plan?

1097. Who can list a Multisourcing Integration project as organization experience, your organization or a previous employee of your organization?

1098. What process manages the contracts?

1099. Describe how often regular updates are made

to the proposed solution. Are corresponding regular updates included in the standard maintenance plan?

1100. How long have you been using the services?

1101. What was the final actual cost?

1102. What are the minimum and optimal bandwidth requirements for the proposed solution?

4.6 Formal Acceptance: Multisourcing Integration

1103. Who supplies data?

1104. Did the Multisourcing Integration project manager and team act in a professional and ethical manner?

1105. What features, practices, and processes proved to be strengths or weaknesses?

1106. What is the Acceptance Management Process?

1107. Was the Multisourcing Integration project managed well?

1108. Does it do what Multisourcing Integration project team said it would?

1109. Was business value realized?

1110. Does it do what client said it would?

1111. Do you buy-in installation services?

1112. Did the Multisourcing Integration project achieve its MOV?

1113. Was the sponsor/customer satisfied?

1114. What lessons were learned about your Multisourcing Integration project management methodology?

1115. Have all comments been addressed?

1116. Was the Multisourcing Integration project work done on time, within budget, and according to specification?

1117. What can you do better next time?

1118. How does your team plan to obtain formal acceptance on your Multisourcing Integration project?

1119. What function(s) does it fill or meet?

1120. Is formal acceptance of the Multisourcing Integration project product documented and distributed?

1121. Do you buy pre-configured systems or build your own configuration?

1122. Who would use it?

5.0 Closing Process Group: Multisourcing Integration

1123. Is this a follow-on to a previous Multisourcing Integration project?

1124. How will you know you did it?

1125. What could be done to improve the process?

1126. What business situation is being addressed?

1127. When will the Multisourcing Integration project be done?

1128. Were sponsors and decision makers available when needed outside regularly scheduled meetings?

1129. How well defined and documented were the Multisourcing Integration project management processes you chose to use?

1130. Did you do things well?

1131. What is the Multisourcing Integration project Management Process?

1132. Are there funding or time constraints?

1133. Just how important is your work to the overall success of the Multisourcing Integration project?

1134. Were risks identified and mitigated?

1135. Were the outcomes different from the already stated planned?

1136. What is the Multisourcing Integration project name and date of completion?

1137. If action is called for, what form should it take?

1138. Mitigate. what will you do to minimize the impact should a risk event occur?

1139. What were the desired outcomes?

5.1 Procurement Audit: Multisourcing Integration

1140. What are the required standards of quality assurance or environmental management?

1141. If a purchase order calls for a cost-plus agreement, is the method of determining how final charges will be determined specified?

1142. Did your organization calculate the contract value accurately?

1143. Did your organization state the minimum requirements to be met by the variants in the tender documents?

1144. Is the departments procurement function/unit well organized?

1145. Is there a policy on making purchases locally where possible?

1146. Were there no inconsistencies between the several tender documents?

1147. When negotiation took place in successive stages, was this practice stated in the procurement documents and was it done in accordance with the award criteria stated?

1148. Were any additional works or deliveries admissible without the need for a new procurement procedure?

1149. Does the strategy ensure that needs are met, and not exceeded?

1150. Has your organization clearly defined the award criteria?

1151. Were the documents received scrutinised for completion and adherence to stated conditions before the tenders were evaluated?

1152. Has your organization fulfilled its obligations related to the payment of social security contributions and taxes?

1153. Are internal control mechanisms performed before payments?

1154. Are there authorizations on file to support all deductions from payroll checks?

1155. Is a risk evaluation performed?

1156. Are required quality and service standards set?

1157. Are proper authorization and approval required prior to payment?

1158. Are the supporting documents for payments voided or cancelled following payment?

5.2 Contract Close-Out: Multisourcing Integration

1159. Parties: who is involved?

1160. Have all contracts been completed?

1161. Was the contract sufficiently clear so as not to result in numerous disputes and misunderstandings?

1162. Was the contract complete without requiring numerous changes and revisions?

1163. Are the signers the authorized officials?

1164. How/when used ?

1165. Have all contracts been closed?

1166. Have all contract records been included in the Multisourcing Integration project archives?

1167. Parties: Authorized?

1168. Was the contract type appropriate?

1169. How does it work?

1170. Change in circumstances?

1171. Have all acceptance criteria been met prior to final payment to contractors?

1172. What happens to the recipient of services?

1173. Change in knowledge?

1174. What is capture management?

1175. Has each contract been audited to verify acceptance and delivery?

1176. How is the contracting office notified of the automatic contract close-out?

1177. Change in attitude or behavior?

5.3 Project or Phase Close-Out: Multisourcing Integration

1178. Who controlled key decisions that were made?

1179. How much influence did the stakeholder have over others?

1180. Who exerted influence that has positively affected or negatively impacted the Multisourcing Integration project?

1181. If you were the Multisourcing Integration project sponsor, how would you determine which Multisourcing Integration project team(s) and/or individuals deserve recognition?

1182. What was expected from each stakeholder?

1183. What process was planned for managing issues/ risks?

1184. What is a Risk Management Process?

1185. In preparing the Lessons Learned report, should it reflect a consensus viewpoint, or should the report reflect the different individual viewpoints?

1186. Does the lesson describe a function that would be done differently the next time?

1187. Was the schedule met?

1188. What is the information level of detail required for each stakeholder?

1189. Is there a clear cause and effect between the activity and the lesson learned?

1190. What hierarchical authority does the stakeholder have in your organization?

1191. Did the delivered product meet the specified requirements and goals of the Multisourcing Integration project?

1192. Was the user/client satisfied with the end product?

1193. What could have been improved?

1194. What are the informational communication needs for each stakeholder?

1195. Is the lesson significant, valid, and applicable?

1196. What are the mandatory communication needs for each stakeholder?

5.4 Lessons Learned: Multisourcing Integration

1197. How will you allocate your funding resources?

1198. What are the influence patterns?

1199. How do security constraints impact the case?

1200. How effective were the communications materials in providing and orienting team members about the details of the Multisourcing Integration project?

1201. How useful was the content of the training you received in preparation for the use of the product/ service?

1202. How long did redeployment take?

1203. How effective was the architecture/system design process?

1204. What are the skills directly related to the task?

1205. What was the geopolitical history during the origin of your organization and at the time of task input?

1206. Is your organization willing to expose problems or mistakes for the betterment of the collective whole, and can you do this in a way that does not intimidate employees or workers?

1207. How clear were you on your role in the Multisourcing Integration project?

1208. Why do you need to measure?

1209. What surprises did the team have to deal with?

1210. What specialization does the task require?

1211. What is below the surface?

1212. How effectively and timely was your organizational change impact identified and planned for?

1213. What is your organizational ideology?

Index

almost 251-252
already   111, 159-160, 224, 260
always 11
Amazon   12
amount   21, 218, 249
amplify64, 114
analysis   3, 6, 13, 64, 67, 71-72, 74-75, 85, 138, 143, 146,
173, 185, 188, 191, 195, 197, 199, 203, 216, 219, 225-226, 232,
238, 249-250
analyze   2, 62, 69, 71, 145, 191
analyzed   103, 162, 211
analyzes   144
another   12, 157, 247
anothers   239
answer 13-14, 18, 30, 47, 62, 79, 95, 107
answered   29, 46, 61, 78, 94, 106, 131
answering   13, 255
anyone   33, 114-115
anything   171, 187, 229-230
appear   1, 175
applicable   14, 101, 179, 195, 229, 255, 266
applied   93, 98, 205, 250
appointed   34, 44
approach   49, 88, 91, 113, 156, 183, 223, 238, 243, 248
approaches   93
approval   38, 121, 236, 262
approvals   147, 155
approve   133, 226
approved   34, 63, 143, 151, 155, 188, 192, 227
approving   151
Architects   8
archived   187
archives   263
around118, 121
arranged   253
arriving161
articulate   248
ascribed   210
asking 1, 8, 194
aspect 244
aspiration   248
assertions   253
assess 26, 39, 101, 108, 220, 225

imbedded   101
immediate   206
impact 5, 43, 50-52, 54, 56, 59, 88, 130, 133, 184, 187-188, 203, 205-209, 222, 226-227, 243, 253, 260, 267-268
impacted   56, 265
impacts   54, 60, 203, 205
implement   27, 52, 71, 95, 225
implicit 125
importance   242
important   19, 40, 68-69, 107-108, 111, 121, 130, 140, 148, 175, 192, 202, 213, 222, 259
improper   231
improve   2, 12-13, 79, 81-82, 85-89, 91-93, 135, 189, 199, 259
improved   83-84, 87, 90, 104, 266
improving   80, 223
inaccurate   147
inactive   183
incentives   102, 241
incident   206, 230
include   28, 82, 146, 163, 195, 199, 215, 225, 238
included   2, 10, 25, 50, 141, 177-178, 186, 215, 226, 255-256, 263
includes   11, 219
including   27, 36-37, 42, 55, 57, 74, 96-97, 104, 208, 242-243, 249
incomplete   147
increase   90, 112
increased   116, 197
increasing   126, 229
incurring   160
in-depth   10, 13
indicate   75, 95, 114
indicated   96
indicators   29, 56, 59, 63, 67, 69, 72, 90, 104, 140, 189
indirect   48, 160, 183
indirectly   1
individual   1, 50, 145, 197, 236, 247-248, 255, 265
induction   254
industry   103, 112, 167
infinite 108
influence   91, 122, 137, 197, 201-202, 213, 229, 265, 267
influences   167

required   19, 27, 33, 38, 40, 44-45, 59, 64, 66, 80, 85, 93,
103, 134, 155, 163-165, 169, 177, 181, 191, 197, 208, 219-220, 245,
261-262, 266
requires   134
requiring   137, 263
research   24, 125, 153, 167, 232-233, 236
Reserve   183
reserved   1
reserves   213
reside 89, 217
resolution   67, 91, 160
resolve 19, 23, 28, 235, 240
resolved   204, 222
Resource   4-5, 141, 146, 161, 165, 171, 173, 176, 199, 203,
218, 224, 236
resourced   231
resources   2, 10, 20-21, 25, 31, 36, 42, 48, 71, 80, 97, 103,
105, 108, 113, 123, 133-134, 138, 143, 146, 153, 164-166, 169, 177,
182, 185, 234, 238, 243, 245, 247, 249, 267
respect   1
respond   140, 237
responded   14
response   24, 95-96, 98-99, 101, 255
responses   90, 108, 205-206, 215-216
responsive   177, 186
result   64, 80, 83, 160, 185, 187, 192, 227, 263
resulted   99
resulting   66, 200
results   10, 32, 36, 69, 79-80, 82, 86-90, 92-93, 99, 104, 133, 140,
144, 162, 165, 175, 183, 185, 190, 221, 246
retain   107, 190
retained   67
retention   52
retrospect   128
return 80, 170, 193-194, 208
returns 191
revenue   21, 54
review 12-13, 33, 72, 169, 182, 206, 225, 230, 236
reviewed   45, 133, 180, 189, 214, 232, 254
reviewer   239
reviews12, 162, 200, 203, 254
revised 68, 99, 232
revisions   263

situations   106, 239
skills   27, 66, 120-121, 129, 187, 196-197, 200, 239, 248, 267
smallest   21, 80
social 239, 262
societal   128
software   28, 141, 150, 161-162, 175-176, 209, 215, 232, 255
solicit   36, 236
solution   52, 66-67, 79, 81-83, 85, 88-91, 95, 256
solutions   81, 83, 89, 93, 99, 205
solved 26
solving 248
Someone   8
someones   239
something   111, 146
sought 138
source 5, 110, 115, 212, 215
sources   41, 70, 72, 150, 207
special 45, 99, 135, 220
specific   10, 22, 37, 44, 67, 130, 145, 156, 163, 165, 171,
173, 198, 222-223, 228, 231, 254
specified   126, 162, 211, 261, 266
specify 238
spoken 107
sponsor   19, 146, 195, 257, 265
sponsors   28, 194, 220, 238, 259
spread 102
stable 148
staffed 42
staffing 27, 102
stages 261
stakes 138
standard   8, 103, 105, 171, 250, 255-256
standards   1, 12-13, 97, 101, 155, 191, 193, 228, 242, 261-262
started 10, 170
starting 13, 141
stated 116, 121, 159-160, 260-262
statement   3, 13, 88, 153, 155-156, 162
statements   14, 29, 36-37, 46, 61, 71, 78, 94, 106, 131, 153, 253
status 5-6, 65, 138, 153, 199-200, 205, 214, 217-218, 223, 234,
251, 255
steady 53
steering   214
storage   194, 226

stories 39
strategic   48, 83, 96, 111, 199-200, 232
strategies   93, 97, 115, 126, 140, 200, 207, 229
strategy   20, 33, 49, 58, 84, 92-93, 104, 117, 119, 123, 131,
156, 161, 249, 262
Stream 65, 70
strength   231
strengths   167, 257
stretch 121
strict   73
strive   121, 221
Strongly   13, 18, 30, 47, 62, 79, 95, 107, 225
structure   3-4, 59, 90, 117, 123, 135, 145, 157, 173, 181, 209,
248
structures   247
stubborn   119
styles   190
subject 10-11, 32
Subjective   192
subjects   76
submit 12, 225
submitted   12, 227-228
subsequent   216
subset 21
succeed   51, 114, 167, 247
success   22-23, 31, 34-35, 39, 44, 50, 55, 60, 82-83, 88, 98,
113-114, 117-119, 122, 135, 153, 162, 169, 181, 224, 229, 242, 245,
259
successes   126
successful   73, 93, 104, 107, 121, 124, 140, 187, 220, 222-223,
245
succession   102
successive   261
sufficient   141
suggest   226, 232
suggested   96, 227
suitable   253-254
summary   176, 195
supplier   123
suppliers   36, 71, 74, 128
supplies   257
supply 53, 167